A CHILD'S WAR
IN CORNWALL

A CHILD'S WAR IN CORNWALL

'THE VOICE OF A SCHOOLBOY'

JOHN C. HARDING

ryelands

First published in Great Britain in 2010

British Library Cataloguing-in-Publication Data
A CIP record for this title is available from the British Library

ISBN 978 1 906551 24 7

RYELANDS
Halsgrove House,
Ryelands Industrial Estate,
Bagley Road, Wellington, Somerset TA21 9PZ
Tel: 01823 653777   Fax: 01823 216796
email: sales@halsgrove.com

Part of the Halsgrove group of companies
Information on all Halsgrove titles is available at: www.halsgrove.com

Printed in Great Britain by The Cromwell Press Group, Wiltshire

CONTENTS

Acknowledgements

Firstly I would like to thank my brother Bob, and sisters Anne and Jean, together with my friends Ted Blackburn and his brother Terry, also Charles Gilbert and Eric Nicholls for memories of the times we shared as children. Meeting them, and their families have given me untold pleasure.

I feel privileged to have Jerry Whitehouse painting on the cover. The boys looking up at the Spitfire are modelled on the artist and his brother, but could quite easily be brothers or friends of many who lived at that time. To me, they are Bob and John Harding.

Thank you Sheilagh for your moving poem 'Turnaware', our chance meeting there on a wet cold day in January was, I believe, arranged.

A very special thank you to my niece Margaret Elliot, who dotted the Is and crossed the Ts for me. Maggie you were my compass.

To my Grandchildren Sam, Harley, Guy and Harry, I say thank you for having patience with an old man and his confounded laptop machine.

To my son Alistair for his never-ending encouragement in my quest to write the book. To my friends John Wood and Jock Huggins for arranging and taking photographs of 'Steep Holm' from the estuary.

For Peter and Elizabeth Newman of Tolverne, a very special thank you not only for their historical photographs, but more, much more, for their dedication and hard work over the years preserving a link for returning veterans who wished to pay homage to their 'Buddies'.

I am grateful to Mr and Mrs Alan Jackson present owners of 'Harbour Lights' ('Steep Holm') forgiving permission from a yacht in the Indian Ocean for me to spend time alone in their property. To think that when we lived there we hadn't ever used a telephone. Thank you Helen and Cyril Harber for arranging it.

It has been my experience that when phoning museums there is always someone ready to give just that little extra help and understanding when asking for permission to publish a photograph. I wish to thank the individuals as well as the establishments, Elizabeth Le Grice and Kim Cooper, of the Cornwall County Library Service, Pauline Allwright, at the Imperial War Museum and all the Staff at the Royal Cornwall Museum, Truro for the photographs of HTP Motors.

A big thank you to Simon Butler and staff at Halsgrove Publishers for everything.

DEDICATION

"I dedicate this book to Children of all Nations who lost their lives as a result of war."

Church Road, Mylor c.1930

Introduction

SETTING THE SCENE

Over sixty-five years have passed since we lived in Cornwall. My family Mum, Dad, sisters Mary, June, Anne, Jean, brother Bob, and myself. Over the years I have often returned to Restronguet Point, Feock, where in five years we grew from children to young adults. Living in such an idyllic area would, at anytime be unforgettable; however, it was war time which adds greatly to the memories we have.

As Mum neared the end of her long life, she liked nothing more than to reminisce about that period in her life she held so dear. On her ninety-eighth birthday I took her back to where she had spent such memorable times. We exchanged our own favourite stories, the happy times shared, and sad times remembered. "Why not write a book, John?" she said, "Tell it as it happened, and write it as it was, from memory. Write it for your grandchildren and their children, of times when we received so little yet had so much."

Mum passed away three years later, I often gave her comments thought but little else – one day perhaps.

I found myself leaning on the gate of the house where we lived – now called 'Harbour Lights' - but it was 'Steep Holm' when we lived there. Dad had named it after the island in the Bristol Channel where he had lived for a short while.

I looked out over the Fal Estuary, as lovely now as it always was; in many parts just exactly the same as the day we left. My mind drifted back over the years and I could almost hear the sounds of Glen Miller's music drifting across the water from ships loaded with men and machinery waiting to cross the Channel, where they would take part in one of the most historic battles in history. I could hear children's laughter as they played, and the deep-throated sound of a Fordson Standard tractor 'labouring' as it pulled a plough.

On the way home I decided 'why not give it a try', who knows, recalling one's childhood might not be a bad thing to do. I've heard it said that everyone has a book inside them worth writing. And in our twilight years, we tend to recall memories of earlier times more vividly than recent events.

So, here are mine. This is a true story of free-range children growing up in war time. Very little research has been carried out, or required; however there has been a lot of reminiscing with those who shared those times, mostly through watery eyes and with a gentle smile.

Often we are asked "How can you remember events from so long ago?" The answer is quite simply, "We never forgot."

John C. Harding
2010

Trams crowd the docks area of old Bristol c.1910

Chapter 1

WHEN I WAS A CHILD

I was eight-and-a-half years old the day war was declared. At the time we were living at 20 Salisbury Avenue Kingswood, Bristol. My father worked at the Douglas Motor Cycle factory at Hanham. He had been a pilot in the RAFVR; however he contacted rheumatic fever and was discharged.

My sisters and I attended Two Mile Hill School, which was just a quarter of a mile from our home. The outbreak of war was no surprise to us, grownups spoke of little else. One of my earliest recollections was, at the age of four, watching a German airship pass over our house at Evesham, where we lived at that time. A passing motor-cyclist stopped at the gate and shouted, "an airship is coming", then continued on down the road to inform others of this rare event.

We went out into a field and watched it pass over. I was fascinated – it was crabbing sideways, swaying in the wind. To see an aeroplane in those days was a thrill, but an airship, that was something special.

The swastika on its tail was the main topic for the grownups, "spying and taking photographs; one day they will bomb London, mark my words."

Dad kept in touch with his squadron, and he took me to an air day at Filton, where three Hurricane fighter aircraft took off in formation, simultaneously lifting their undercarriages, the highlight of the day for me. I was lifted into the cockpit of a biplane that had its engine running, the pilot fired the machine gun into a sandbag wall. I didn't like that one bit. On the way home Dad's pals were full of 'doom and gloom' "they will slaughter us," they said. Dad made up his mind that day, *when* war came – not, *if* – we would move, and to make light of it he winked and added "to the coast".

War or no war, if we were going to move to the coast – or anywhere else for that matter – the sooner the better for me. The reason was that the

Headmaster at Two mile Hill school was a bully with a capital 'B'.

Mum was fanatical regarding our health, doctors and medicines cost money. A man would call on Saturday mornings to collect weekly payments for past treatments, and so good health paid dividends in more ways than one.

I was force-fed cabbage, and drank the water it was cooked in; all of us were given 'jollop' by the spoonful – Parishes' Food, Virol, Scots' Emulsion; you name it we had it: "Open your mouth this is good for you".

Thursday nights of all nights (why not on a Friday?), chocolate laxative, needed or not, before bed. Halfway to school the next day I needed the toilet; there was little time to spare, nothing for it but to return home. Ten minutes later I arrived at school, five minutes late, the head was standing at the gate, watch in one hand cane in the other. I started to explain but he was having none of it; he had heard more excuses than he could remember, and I was about to find out why he was called the 'right-hand man'. Five of us lined up, four 'old hands' and myself, a first timer. I was the last one in line. Swish, crack, the first boy staggered off holding his hand under his armpit. Down the head came, raising the cane above his head, and – believe it, or not – stood on his toes, to get a longer sweep. My turn. I didn't cry but I needed the toilet. I hold the honour of being the last boy caned before the war at Two Mile Hill School Kingswood, on Friday 1 September 1939.

The following Sunday at eleven o'clock, I sat outside our house on my bicycle, dressed in short trousers, pullover and a cap. I was alone, no cars, or people, just silence. England held its breath; millions listened to the wireless, mostly sharing with neighbours, twiddling the tuning knob, hoping to get a better reception, until at eleven o'clock those historic words, were heard by a waiting nation: "We are at war with Germany."

A 1928 Wolseley Saloon.

For reasons I have forgotten, I didn't hear the historic broadcast, just sitting alone, outside No. 20, one foot resting on the peddle, the other on the curb, alone with my thoughts; war was a 'grown-ups' thing, just go along with it.

I remember riding off to find my friends; there would be cigarette cards to swap in the shed on the allotments. After dinner, as the midday meal was called then, we had a treat, our first trip in the car. Dad had bought it on the roadside from a couple who had broken down. It was a Wolseley, a 1928 model, and he paid ten pounds for it, as seen. The couple seemed very pleased to get shot of it, and we were soon to find out why!

All-aboard, we were off to Burnham-on-Sea to visit Gran and Granddad Hunt. The girls sat in the back on deep, tanned leather seats. Mum, with Bob on her lap, sat next to Dad. I stood up behind the driver, who, as usual was singing 'Tom Bowling'.

On we motored down the A38 , until we came to a straight road; foot down on the accelerator 27, 29 then 30mph. Screams from the back, a shout from Mum, "what's up Jimmy". The singing stopped the car shook; we had suddenly acquired square wheels. Pulling into the side of the road, Dad got out – he was an engineer this shouldn't take long. Kicking each wheel in turn he got back in. "Seems ok" he said. Mum mumbled something about ten pounds, Dad twiddled his moustache, we were off again. "Hold tight I will take

her through the barrier, whatever that was – 28, 30mph shake, lots of it. Leaning over the seat it was impossible to read the speedo due to the needle vibrating – 34, settling down now, 36. "Slow down Jimmy." 31, 30, shake... shake. Then we were on the grass verge. "Everyone get out and push".

In the months that followed Dad always tried to get the car up 60mph to see if the shaking reappeared, however she just would not have it (I am referring to the car!).

Naturally the outbreak of war was the main topic at Burnham-on-Sea. Granddad didn't think that any of us would live to see the end of it, and that the young ones – us – should be sent to Canada. This was too much gloom and doom for us, and we ran along the beach where defence preparations were already in hand: telegraph posts being dug into the sand to prevent the landing of troop-carrying gliders. We had that day not a care in the world; we watched model boats sailing on the pond, swimmers in the lido, spent our penny pocket money – I lost mine in a slot machine. All in all a good day at the sea side, this, the first day of war.

In the weeks that followed, gas masks were issued – then returned for modification – a second filter taped to the end. Blackout was enforced, an

On 3 September 1939 at Burnham-on-Sea. Back row: June, Gran and Mary. Front row: 'the gang', first left Anne, Bob, John and Jean.

Anderson shelter was installed in the garden, which filled, almost at once, with a foot of water. Despite bailing it out, the water always returned, and the shelter was never usable, not that we ever put it to the test.

Much to Dad's disappointment he was turned down for RAFVR service. However he was offered, and accepted, a post as an inspector for fighter aircraft repair. This new position required that he move to Plymouth, which caused him some anxiety regarding our well being. He would have greater peace of mind if we moved to a safer area, and with this thought uppermost in his mind, a tenancy on a cottage at Berrow, near Burnham-on-Sea, was agreed. There was one snag, Mum, for reasons best known to herself, flatly refused to live there.

Dad said that we were moving, Mum that we were not. 'High Noon' was a Saturday. School had been informed that we were leaving, goodbyes had been said, but my sisters and I were between the 'devil and the deep-blue sea.'

The removal van and three men arrived, and news had spread throughout the avenue, so a small crowd had gathered, a lasting memory was in the making.

First the kitchen table was carried out and an argument developed between our parents as to who was the legal owner. The kitchen table was carried back into the house. The piano was next. Mum had always boasted "It's German, you know, and it has an iron frame." Voices were raised. Dad's cousin had given it to Mum.

Avenue Amateur Attorneys all gave their two penny's worth of advice as to who was the rightful owner. Mum's red hair was getting redder, the crowd was getting bigger. Dad gave a speech, "As a child in the Great War," he said "I saw the effects of bombing in London. Believe me; this time it will be much worse. I am to move away in order to do my bit, and wish my family to be as safe as possible." There were cheers, there were boos.

The removal men unloaded the furniture into the garden, "Please let us know when this war is over, and terms have been agreed," they said.

On Monday we went back to school. There would be times in the not too distant future when Mum would regret the stance she had taken; equally, no doubt, Dad would be more than happy with the way things turned out.

In the path of life we all arrive at a fork in the road, and the decision as to which direction is taken, will have lasting implications, left or right, the high road, the low road, North or South, there are bound to be new friends, and interests. On a normally quiet Saturday morning, in a normally quiet avenue in Kingswood Bristol, unknown to any of us at the time, a decision was made on our behalf by something or someone that would have a major influence on the rest of our lives. Mum often spoke of that day. "I never truly understood why I didn't want to return to the area where I had grown up."

Ironically when peace finally returned we would move to within one mile of Berrow.

Life returned to normal, I gave up piano lessons, or to be more exact, lessons gave up me; the teacher called and said that, I didn't know as much after two years, as I did the day I had started.

At school an announcement was made that the Headmaster was leaving to join the army. George Butt, my best friend, whispered, "I hope the Germans cut his willy off," which almost made me the last boy to be caned by the head for, 'laughing loudly in assembly'.

We watched the troops passing down Two Mile Hill leaving for France, we had our last ice cream, (for seven years), or at least an ice lolly made by Walls, a three-corner shaped one in a cardboard tube; it cost, three-farthings. The next one would be in 1947.

The weather was colder then; we had snow every year. Ice would form on the inside of our bedroom windows. We would run down the bank in St George's Park, jump on the ice, and slide across. Boys, and possibly girls too, had chaps on top of their ears; we would pick the scabs off and make them bleed. We had a third of a pint of milk at school – cost, half a penny. I don't remember the total number of pupils attending Two Mile Hill School at that time. However if it was, say, 480, the total cost of the milk each day, for the whole school would have been, one pound.

During school holidays, milk was still available, if ordered. One teacher would be in attendance. The top third of the bottle would be cream. Every one of us would lick the cardboard tops. Cows were brown then, not black and white. Funny how we remember such things.

A lady sold bananas outside her front door in St George's. One day Mum, stopped on the way home from the park, bought seven, the total stock. They were the last ones we would have for five years.

Christmas 1939 was for us, the most memorable of our childhood. The truth is that the future for children everywhere looked uncertain, we were spoilt. It's the out-of-the-ordinary events that are remembered, the unexpected, the spontaneous; we have all had them, and this is one of mine.

As part of the blackout; buses, and trams, were fitted with pale blue lights, bright enough to find one's seat, not bright enough to be spotted from the air.

It was Christmas Eve at No.20, the excitement was electric. It was seven o'clock in the evening and we were having a bath on the kitchen table. "Father Christmas likes clean children," Mum said. June was ready for bed and was getting a little impatient: "I will have a look outside". There was a scream, in she dashed, up the stairs, two or even three steps at a time, shouting "he's here, I saw him."

"How could you see him in the blackout?" was shouted back as I jumped out of the bath grabbing a towel."

"He has a blue light on top of his head," was the stern reply – as if we should know such things. "Why?"

June came halfway down the stairs leaned over the banister, "So that the Germans won't see him."

I cannot remember who said it, I wish it was me: "Will he take it off when he gets to Germany?"

Over the Christmas period we visited our grandparents at Clevedon. Grandpa Harding had worked at The Ministry of Health in London, and had retired early. Over the years he had travelled the world with Grandma, and for this reason we had not enjoyed their company as often as they, or ourselves, would have liked. At the outbreak of hostilities they returned home. To say we were spoilt by them that Christmas would be an understatement.

Despite the fact it was Christmas, the conversation was the war, and our future. It was very apparent that there was a lot of support for Granddad Hunt's idea that we should go to Canada. Mum was having none of it, many children had lost their lives due to ships being sunk, and Canada was a long way away, and so on.

A conversation between Grandpa Harding and myself has always intrigued me. We were sitting together by the fire while the ladies were doing things that ladies do at Christmas time. Dad and his sister Aunt Peggy, were discussing the pro's and con's of turning a car engine off when travelling downhill 'to save petrol'. Grandpa handed me a book, "Read this, John," he said. "I have read it," he continued, "I had a dream about it, the main character was played by you. It was most uncanny, so real"

A short while later Grandpa was walking through London. Men were unloading large oak barrels from a dray, the horses were frightened by something and a barrel rolled off and hit him. He died shortly afterwards.

The book, *Jack Harding's Quest*, relates the adventures of boys living in Cornwall. It tells of rocky coves, white sandy beaches, and caves, with the odd smuggler thrown in for good measure. As we will see, Grandpa's dream was uncanny.

Dad moved to Plymouth. War, for us at least, was, quiet; there were no air-raid warnings as such, just practice; in fact very little in the way of action.

At that time most items in Woolworths cost sixpence, or less. I had a 'Frog' model aircraft with and elastic-driven propeller, and a winding mechanism built into its box. It cost, sixpence.

In a shop on the main street there was a Schuco model clockwork car. It had four gears, plus reverse, steering, and a handbrake. Made in Germany, the price, four shillings and eleven pence halfpenny. By the time I had saved enough birthday, Christmas and weekly pocket money, the staff had all joined up and the shop was closed. Fifty years later I bought a similar model at an auction; it cost me eighty-five pounds.

Salisbury Avenue, was reasonably flat, ideal for our Saturday sport, hockey; not the normal run of the mill stuff, this was played on roller skates with ball-bearing wheels – a game for boys resulting in bruised knees, played with wooden sticks and a tin can.

Cars were few and far between, we didn't stop for them, and they didn't slow down for us. Horses waiting for the baker or milkman to return from deliveries, watched the game over their nose bags. There was no referee, those who shouted the loudest won the point. Trolleys were a status symbol then, I had a three-wheeler with a sail, more of a sand yacht than a trolley.

Marbles were both collected and played with; one foot on the curb-stone, the other in the gutter. We played on the way home from school, parked cars were no hazard – there were no parked cars!

Five years ago I had reason to go to Bristol and I decided to go to the area where we had spent those early war years. With only half a mile left to go I changed my mind, and turned around. The memories I have are of friends, not of new buildings, and busy roads. Not that I am saying it was better then, seventy years ago. However, as we grow older, our most precious gift is one's memory.

The furniture van was loaded to capacity. This time it was for real, goodbyes had been said, we were moving to Plymouth. There was not enough room in the van for the trolley which was the envy of every boy in the avenue. He stood there watching, aged about seven years old; he was always there early on Saturday mornings standing by the gate. I cannot give him a name because I never knew it, he was one of a large family who lived around the corner; his eldest sister had died at the age of fourteen with what must have been leukaemia. She was a friend of Mary and June and after her death, he just attached himself to us; standing by the gate, watching.

Many attempts had been made to get closer to him without success. I looked at Dad who looked at him, then at the trolley parked on the pavement, "Would you like it, son," Dad said. Just a nod nothing more. We left him there just standing on the pavement holding the steering rope, waiting.

Chapter 2

PLYMOUTH

'Dorothea' is an Edwardian semi detached house in Elburton Road, Plymstock – it is still there, its name changed – on the main Kingsbridge to Plymouth Road. It had three bedrooms and – for us – a luxury, electricity.

The rear garden had no marked boundary as such, at the bottom there was a copse, running through which was a single railway track serving a local quarry. Beyond this, a hill and shrubland mainly covered with gorse bushes. From the small front garden there was a view of Plymouth, approximately two miles away.

I attended Goosewell School Plymstock, and was very happy there making a lot of friends. War and

its progress – or lack of it – was incorporated into general subjects such as geography and history; the British Empire in particular. A large map hung on the classroom wall with the colonies shown in pink. The size of the British Empire in comparison to Germany gave us encouragement as to the final outcome of the war. Even then in 'the darkest hour' we were bound to win; for children there never was any doubt as to the final outcome.

Each morning our teacher gave us an update of the situation, tapping the map with a stick, pointing to areas where news, and history, was being made.

All news items were censored. Where things were not looking good, coverage was kept to a minimum. Evacuation of Commonwealth forces from the beaches at Dunkirk was one such

The road from Elburton to Plymouth c.1945. On the right is the entrance to Plymstock station.

example. Ships of all sizes, were ferrying troops, who had been trapped on the beaches, back across the English Channel. This was the news of the day. I stood up, "Sir," I said, holding up a pocket watch which had stopped at ten past eight, "This watch was in the pocket of my next door neighbour when he boarded a ship after wading into the sea. I asked him if I could bring it to show my friends."

Each member of the class held an item of historical significance, an up to date hands-on history lesson, and we each held the watch which recorded the time when England held its breath.

On Sundays we would often take a picnic to Wembury, spending the day exploring pools, swimming, or looking out to sea. This was to all intent and purposes a battle zone, looking out at ships and aircraft engaged in war. Gunfire could be heard way out at sea. On one occasion we saw two naval ships dropping depth charges; it could have been practice of course, there was no way of knowing – the ships were real and so were the white columns of water astern.

It was from here that we had our first sight of the enemy, a twin-engine German bomber flying out from the direction of Plymouth, leaving a trail of black smoke. It flew like a ship passing over waves, continually climbing then falling, slowly losing height, as it did so. The crew must have bailed out before it came into our view, we saw nothing of them. Crashing into the sea, the aircraft quickly disappeared. Dad went off to inform someone but I doubt if he was the first to do so.

From Wembury we saw the arrival of American First World War destroyers; part of a Lend Lease agreement between Great Britain and The United States. They looked dated, steaming in line. A Sunderland flying boat flew low overhead.

Workmen were constructing pill boxes – on a Sunday – barbed wire stretched along the shore. There was an opening to allow access for the public, but in order that the gap could be closed at short notice a large coil of barbed wire was at hand. Preparations were going ahead at full speed,

The location of this photograph is not known with any certainty, but more than likely it was taken at Wembury in the summer of 1940. This was to be the last family photograph taken for seven years.

with as little interference to civilians as possible. I say with all honesty we were never throughout all the war years told, 'this far and no farther'. It goes without saying that if there was a sentry on duty it was a 'no go area'. However as a general rule we were free to roam.

He stood on the shore at Wembury, alone, just looking out to sea, dressed in civilian clothes, wearing a suit and black shoes. As we watched he bent down placing a stone on the water's edge then, stepping back, he returned to looking at the horizon, another stone and so on. Intrigued, Dad, Bob, and I casually strolled down the beach, and stood at the water's edge just a few feet away from him.

"I'm from Canada." he said. "This is the first time I have ever seen the ocean. He just looked out to sea, wonderful, alive, moving in and out, and slowly creeping up the shore. He paused taking, a deep breath, "The smell," everything about it is different than I imagine. Which direction is Canada?"

Dad pointed towards Plymouth Sound, "Canada's a big country," he said, "it lies in that general direction about three thousand miles, away, you would make landfall on its East coast."

Bob asked if he was going to swim home. "No Sir, I only arrived here last night".

He took his shoes and socks off, joining us in what must have been his first paddle in salt water, after which we all had a sandwich. He didn't say, and we didn't ask, why he was in England, this was a time of 'careless talk costs lives'. My guess was that he would soon be flying in a Sunderland flying boat over the Atlantic Ocean, looking down at more ocean than he had ever dreamt of, thinking of home and of snow-covered mountains.

Few Children at that time had money to spend, the age-old custom of bartering was the name of the game. For those of you who are not familiar with the finer points and skills required, I will try to explain. It is little more than a mixture of, knowing the value of the item you wish to get rid of, combined with the overwhelming desire to

The French liner Normandie.

own a particular gem. On offer that day was a solid silver cigarette lighter made from two table-spoons. It was very well made, finely engineered, with fitted covers top and bottom.

Cigarette lighters at that time were in vogue, most made from .303 rifle cartridges; we all had one. One drawback of the one of offer was that its vendor knew its bargaining value, and there was some playground interest. Each day a more attractive item was offered, and rejected.

Just before the outbreak of hostilities, the French liner *Normandie* visited Plymouth. Regrettably I hadn't seen her, while most of the boys at school had, and fell in love with this beautiful vessel. I owned a Bassett Lowke waterline model of her – acquired from a previous barter. Finer details were pointed out to the owner of the cigarette lighter: the clipper bow, three solid-looking raked funnels, previous holder of the 'Blue Riband' and so on. I could have saved the sales patter, he was hooked, chewing his bottom lip, pulling his ear, he was eager to swap and the lighter was soon in my pocket while he owned the model, box and all.

Over the next few years, and who knows beyond, that silver lighter became a lucky charm, a St Christopher-like superstition perhaps, but in traumatic times children – and as we will see adults – often needed something to hold on to, and those were such times.

A Sunderland flying boat on take off.

We also had the occasional day out at Cawsand, after walking to Hooe and boarding an open motor ferry, which carried about twelve passengers. The trip took us very close to RAF Mountbatten, which gave us a good view of the Sunderland flying boats, both on the slipway and on their moorings. The Australian airmen often returned our greetings as they prepared for their next patrol, hunting U-boats and escorting convoys.

Once or twice we were lucky enough to watch as one of these graceful flying boats took off. What a sight, the hull slowly lifting off the sea, then climbing, water dripping from the hull.

But by far the most memorable sight was 'The day of the *Hood*,' one which, those privileged enough to have witnessed it, will never have

forgotten. Sometimes referred to as HMS *Hood*, but nearly always just as the *Hood*, either way there is just a short pause after her name is spoken. HMS *Hood* – the *Hood* – and why not, she was the pride of the free world. Hitler was afraid of her, and any plans he had at that time to invade this country by sea, the *Hood*, and of course the Royal Navy, would have been a major stumbling block.

Wartime morale was based around this vessel, particularly so by children, so one can imagine our excitement. She was steaming out of Devonport and the skipper of the ferry slowed down, almost stopping as she passed by. We were close enough to wave to the crew on the decks, as from her forward funnel black smoke drifted back towards the Hoe. Her powerful engines stirred up the sediment of Plymouth Sound as she steamed out past the breakwater. How could we not win the war when we had such powerful ships? She was the largest in the world.

Ashore at Cawsand we swam and played on the beach. One day stands out in our memories when we were exploring a group of rocks, and Dad was with us. A man standing at the water's edge shouted a warning to us that the tide was coming in, but Dad was sure the tide was ebbing, and told him so. Time passed, both Anne and I were convinced that the sea was getting deeper.

HMS Hood *seen beyond a Sunderland flying boat lying moored in Plymouth Sound. Two months after this photograph was taken this mighty battlecruiser was blown up and most of her crew lost.*

However contradiction of parents was just not done, and besides we were enjoying ourselves. Anne, Jean and Bob could not swim, and there was not a lot of time to learn, sea had replaced rocks.

The chap who had warned us returned, he had two local fishermen with him and they waded out, the water up to their waists, lifting the young ones on their shoulders. In no time we were back on the beach where a small crowd had gathered. Our adventure was never mentioned again, well not in Dad's presence!

Plymouth, from late 1940, experienced the occasional air raid, one or two during daylight hours, others at night. During one such attack, the oil tanks at Turnchapel were set on fire. A black plume of smoke lifted into the sky and continued doing so for days. The glow was so bright at night that it was possible to go out into the road outside our house and read a newspaper.

As a precaution from the risk of an explosion, many of my schoolfriends were evacuated from their homes at Hooe. One day an unexploded bomb went off near our school. We were just about to have our lunch, the young lady teacher was pouring hot water into a mug which contained an Oxo cube. This, together with two slices of bread, would have been my lunch, had it not ended up on the floor!

Bob and I were playing near the railway line behind the house. Our neighbour had given us an air rifle and we were firing at a target pinned to a tree. Suddenly a man dressed in a light brown boiler suit, slid down the bank on the opposite side, just twenty feet away from us. He seemed just as surprised to see us as we were to see him. We just stood there looking at him, he in turn, looking at us. Not a word was spoken, two fair-haired children, one five years old the other ten,

Schoolboys look on as the oil tanks burn at Turnchapel.

holding a gun, and him – although we never found out for certain – was, by the look of his suit, an airman, and a German to boot. Shouting from the rough ground beyond broke the silent deadlock that had developed between one desperate-to-escape Jerry, and two children, both of whom were fast running out of courage. With one last look at us, he ran off up the line.

The pursuers came through the same gap as the pursued had done just minutes before, three were dressed in khaki battledress, a dog handler in blue serge. He had control of the dog, or to be more precise the dog had control of him, as it came straight at us, dragging the fellow in the blue suit. The angry looking dog's teeth were inches away from my bare legs. Now I am as patriotic as the next, but if you want the truth, I preferred the German to the dog.

We hadn't moved one inch throughout the whole episode, we just stood there speechless pointing in the direction of where the man had gone, and I cannot remember if anything was said or not.

Bob was the first one to find his voice, "That was a German, we should have pointed the gun at him."

"Next time 'Bruv', I will give you the gun." I replied.

He may not have been a German, an escaped prisoner from Dartmoor perhaps, but to us with his light brown boiler suit, he was an airman. There never was any feedback during the war years, what we saw was all we knew. Over the years, since the time covered by this book, memories, such as the one just recalled, and others in the following chapters, are deliberated over. We, just children, had eye-to-eye contact with a man, whose fellow countrymen would be responsible for killing hundreds of thousands of children of our age, and yet very soon his family would be informed that he was 'missing over England', and no doubt, they would ask God "Please take care of him," and as we will hear, just a short while into the future, we too would ask that same God, "Please take care of us".

A road block had been erected a little way down the road near our house. Pyramid-shaped concrete tank barriers and sand bags protected a sentry box which was manned twenty-four hours per day. Traffic had to stop and identity cards had to be shown before zigzagging through. This gave us time to record passing car number plates, a favourite pastime, with the record for one day being fifty-eight numbers. Buses towed trailers with gas-filled bags, used as fuel instead of scarce petrol. Some cars had the same arrangement, but in their case storage was on the roof.

Unlike Salisbury Avenue, we were not provided with an Anderson shelter. A pamphlet was issued, explaining the best area in the house for optimal protection. Some families chose under the stairs, others under the table in a metal cage-like structure; there was no set pattern, each to their own.

Dad opted for the cellar, in an area behind concrete steps that led down into the garden; here there was an eight foot barrier against bomb blast. The floor area of the cellar was perhaps fifty square feet, on two levels; a two-foot-six-inch-high wall divided the lower area from the top, this tapering away to nothing under the house.

In the hallway above a trapdoor was cut for easy and quick entry or exit. A door led into the garden, thus giving two emergency exits in the event of fire or building collapse.

A removable barrier was placed behind the cellar door, consisting of partly-filled sandbags, light enough to lift clear and yet large enough to protect us from blast, along with bags of coal and a large cast-iron mangle.

The plan rested on the assumption that, in the event of fire and an emergency evacuation, there would be a choice of two exits, the cellar door into the garden, or through the trapdoor then out through the front door.

The shelter was just about ready when, Dad was informed he was being transferred to Truro in Cornwall with immediate effect. We spent the next day, at Dad's insistence, carrying out 'dummy' runs in the shelter, each of us being made responsible for an individual task: Mary and June bedding off the beds and down the hatch, Anne and Jean towels and first aid equipment, Bob get himself down the hatch and out the way, plus helping if requested, yours truly, to light candles and primus stove away from the shelter area. Mum was responsible for emergency rations.

Our parents were put into a tightrope situation. On the one hand we had to behave responsibly, while on the other we were somewhat shielded from reality. The truth was that many large cities in England were being blitzed. Devonport was a major naval base and our turn would undoubtedly come, and we were told in the rare event to make sure of this or that.

We had watched changes from peace time to war from the sidelines as it were, never being directly involved. We had taken shortages and the non-existence of certain items in our stride, now we were about to see the reality of this 'grown-ups war.'

Dad left for Truro but life continued on. A Lysander light aircraft landed in a nearby field, took on board two men dressed in civilian clothes then took off again.

Mary had her first boyfriend, Sidney Burns (I hope that is the correct spelling), and she was teased remorselessly by her brothers and sisters. Her first diary recorded her happiness; every entry was the same, "I went for a walk with Sidney Burns."

In those days the entrance exam for grammar school was taken in two parts, passing the first, entitled sitting the second, there being about one month between the two.

Passing the first part didn't create a problem; life for me could not have been better, good school, excellent teachers, and the very best of friends.

Before the blitz in Plymouth, 1937, shows a busy and prosperous city with the streets bedecked for the celebration of King George VI's Coronation.

Chapter 3

THE STORM

The day at school was very much like any other, except that their Majesties the King and Queen paid a visit to Plymouth. After school, for an unexplained reason (it was not as I recall intuition, just a spur of the moment decision), I decided that I would turn left at Billicombe road instead of right. On I went alone; I can only think that my reasons for doing so were in the hope of seeing their Majesties. Passing cars, buses, horses and carts I went on over the bridge, crossing the river Plym, no sign of crowds, on to the Barbican heading towards the Hoe.

While walking along the narrow streets, where buildings overhung the road below, a lady who was standing in a shop doorway, asked with a smile "Where are you going, son"?

"To see the King and Queen, could you please tell me where I can find them?" I asked.

"They've gone back to London on the train. Where do you live?"

I told her, and she said "I'm going that way," adding "it will soon be dark."

Darkness then with the blackout would have been just that, dark. We walked and chatted for a while, the lady and I, she wearing strong smelling perfume, me with a gas mask slung over my shoulder. We met two policemen and she spoke to them about me. The lady smiled then turned and walked slowly back towards the city centre. As I grew up and became more 'worldly wise' I often thought of that lady who more than likely saved my life.

The taller of the two policemen took over my wellbeing and, as I was escorted as far as the bridge, we chatted. "In two hours time I will be off duty, then, home," he said.

"Did you see the King and Queen I enquired?"

"Yes, I did."

On we went the two of us through the narrow streets and past old buildings which had stood the test of time. Tomorrow many would be just rubble.

Reaching the bridge we parted company, after receiving strict instructions from the policeman to "go straight home" I turned and waved, behind him rose the skyline of the city. I very much doubt if he went home that night.

It was dusk as I arrived home; Mum was in the front garden with my brother and sisters, who were talking to Sidney Burns, Mary's sweetheart; the sentries were outside their hut.

We all just chatted, there seemed no urgency on that spring evening, memories perhaps playing tricks. All I can remember is the eerie silence, no aircraft overhead or cars passing by. I look back as if in a dream; the world just stood still, the old city of Plymouth and her people waiting in anticipation.

A flare appeared high up in the sky to the southeast, floating slowly down to earth, it glowed for what seemed an eternity, and then in the distance we could hear the sound of aircraft.

We were shaken back to reality with a jolt. Many times we had heard sirens which were located around the area; when sounding a warning several could be heard at the same time, never in harmony, some rising in pitch others falling. Not this time, they sounded as one, loud, clear, and meaningful, as if to say 'listen to us, this is for real'. The high notes were higher than normal, the low notes lower and prolonged.

Mum could not hide her anxiety, she knew the burden of responsibility rested with her, and the sound of aircraft could now be heard – lots of them – searchlights were scanning the skies. Turning to Sidney she said, "I think you had better run along home, son".

There was a chorus of pleas, asking if he could stay, "No, his mummy will be frantic with worry."

There was no way we could contact his mother, just for a split second Mary and Sidney's eyes met.

We watched as he ran through the road barrier, silhouetted against the glow from fires that had already started, then he was gone. We never saw or heard anything of him again.

Each one of us knew the role we had to play, and this time it was for real. In no time at all everything was in place. June and I had one last look out of the front door, tracer shells were curving into the sky, flashes were seen from anti-aircraft guns and bombs.

The kettle was boiling, mugs of cocoa were handed around; it was going to be a long night. We were all in one corner of the cellar, behind the steps and wall. Anne, Jean and Bob were lying on a mattress covered up under an eiderdown made by Granddad Hunt from suit patterns. Mum sat between Mary and June, and I was opposite facing them and the door.

The main attack seemed to be over the city, some way off. We could hear German aircraft passing over us, there seemed to be a pattern, coming in over Plymouth Sound, dropping their bombs, and then turning east passing overhead.

We settled down and chatted, nervous talk, each trying to convince the others that they were not afraid. We made the odd drink, had a slice of homemade cake; I had forgotten how hungry I was, not having eaten since midday. We played 'I-spy', stopping when an aircraft flew low overhead. We thought of Dad too – we didn't know then but the glow of the fires at Plymouth could be seen from as far away as Truro.

I wanted to go up the ladder and have a look outside, making lots of excuses, "shall I get the gramophone"? We only had one record, 'The Laughing Policeman', which Dad had often said, "It's been played so many times, it's worn that thin it plays both sides at once!" Always the answer to my request to go upstairs was "Let's wait until this quietens down."

At about one o'clock the bombing and gunfire stopped. Mum whispered, "Give it five minutes, if it's still quiet we will go up and have a look." Our water supply was getting low.

We could still hear the droning of aircraft engines, lots of them, and getting closer. The ground shook under the fierce fury of the aerial bombardment.

Of course we had no idea what type of aircraft they were. However from the high-pitched screaming of their engines I would say that there were Stuka dive bombers as well as the heavier two-engined types. We could plainly hear the bombs whistling, and they were getting closer. June had a handkerchief in her hand chewing the corner of it, as she quietly sobbed. "I read in the paper that if you can hear the whistle the bomb will not fall near." She was half talking half sobbing, her words, intended to give moral support. For a short while it helped, however the whistling was continuous, the explosions nonstop, I was cold, and shaking. Mum leaned towards me, "Blow out some of the candles son." I knew it was to hide the tears that were running down her cheeks, and as I did as requested. I pulled down the eiderdown covering my brother and two younger sisters; Anne immediately grabbed it, pulling it back over them. Bob's eyes were closed, his teeth were chattering.

In the semi-darkness I started to quietly recite the Lord's Prayer. However the nearness of the explosions interrupted my concentration, and two or three times I had to restart from the beginning Mary June, and Mum, joined in. I don't recall hearing the whistles, just the violent explosions as the bombs hit the earth.

The city in flames. A photograph of Plymouth taken on the night of the 20 March 1941.

How can our memories record traumatic events in a split second, store them where they will not hurt for the rest of our lives, yet recall them in an instant when triggered. Fifty years after the war a shotgun was fired very near to my sister Jean, and the smell of cordite brought back to her the following events in every detail.

There is no sequence here, it all happened at once. A flash of light came down the open hatch. The mangle, bags of coal and sandbags flew across the cellar, together with the door. The mangle smashed against the wall, breaking its cast iron frame into two or three pieces, the smell of coal dust, musty plaster, and cordite filled the air. The last of the candles went out, there was no door, just an empty space, and we could clearly see the flashes as they lit up the cellar. There was the sound of breaking of glass and items from the rooms above. I felt a burning sensation under my right eye. We could see incendiary bombs glowing brightly in the garden; one must have hit the roof and we could hear it sliding down the tiles

The raid continued, although incendiary bombs had to some extent replaced the explosive type. We could hear them hissing as they burnt, not unlike sparklers on bonfire night.

There was loud knocking at the front door. My elder sisters were asked to watch over the others, Mum and I went up the ladder to answer the front door. The air raid warden stepped straight into the hallway, it was clear to see he had been through a busy night. "You will have to move out, there's an unexploded bomb in your back garden."

How he knew it was there I have never been able to fathom out, and there wasn't time, then, to ask.

"Where shall we go?" asked Mum.

"Anywhere" he said frustratingly.

The city was burning from end to end. German aircraft could still be heard low overhead and incendiary bombs were glowing all around. Mum was being ordered, perhaps advised forcefully would be a more appropriate phrase, for our safety, to take her family out into the thick of it.

"I have six children here, come and see." Together, the three of us went and looked down the hatch, shining a torch where white eyes looked up from blackened faces. The Air Raid Warden's words were repeated by Mum in the

years that followed, more times than I care to remember. "Poor little buggers, leave them there, but do not allow them to go up into the house." He had gambled with the chances of the bomb not going off. He was one of many unsung heroes that night.

Mum and I went into the kitchen to restock supplies; a glow could be seen outside the back door and there was a smell of burning paint. It all happened so fast, Mum grabbed a towel, put it over the door handle, opened it and stepped out.

There it was, an incendiary bomb lying on the top step, on fire. Mum kicked it off the steps down into the garden. Swear words were not heard then, at least not from our parents, however Mum uttered the very same swear word that the warden had used just moments before, which no doubt still echoed in her mind: "Get down there you bugger".

And then, its the spur of the moment humour that's always the funniest (and remembered the longest); pushing me she said "Get in quick John, we mustn't show a light." The world was on fire out there, and we mustn't show a light! The humour of her comment wasn't lost, she put her arm around my shoulder, we laughed, and perhaps cried a little, relief of pent-up fear no doubt. There was an unexploded bomb lying in the garden, our faces were black with dust, half the roof tiles were missing, a large chunk was out of the side of the house, blood was running down my cheek and Mum and I were laughing. Memories don't come greater than that.

The all clear siren sounded a long way off on that cold spring morning, the sound drifting in through a gap where just hours before a door had been, coming from a once proud City, now blanketed in smoke and lying in ruins.

A burnt smell mixed with the aftermath of high explosives and incendiary bombs filled the air. Was it the all clear siren we could hear? Or was it, as now remembered by an old man, a solo trumpeter playing the 'Last Post' for the many hundreds who had lost their lives that night. Or perhaps it was a lament from a burned-out church organ, softly playing 'The Day Thou Gave Us Lord Has Ended.'?

In that year, 1941, 926 civilians lost their lives in Plymouth, of these 227 were children, plus others who at sixteen years of age, served with the Civil Defence, where a total of 41 were lost.

Each member of our family had separate experiences the following day, ranging from frightening, to downright stupidity.

Let's start with the latter, get it over with, Me. First light, the others were sleeping, Bob and I crept out of the gap where the door had been the day before. We had recovered from the trauma of the raid, we were safe, it was now adventure time. An unexploded bomb the warden had said, let's find it. We did, or at least we found the hole it had made, and we stood over it looking down, nothing but earth. And to cap it all, it wasn't even in our garden, it was just on the edge of the copse and next door's boundary, about forty feet from our house. Caught red-handed, the bomb disposal team arrived. Had we kept our mouths shut, and gone back into the cellar, we would have got away with it, but we ran out to meet them, "Would you like us to show you where it is?" we said.

To be fair they had been up all night, their nerves must have been like coiled springs, but all five of them shouting at once, was a bit over the top, anyone would think we had thrown rocks at it, listening to them.

After the bomb had been defused and hoisted out of the ground, the 'squad', took us to have a look at it lying on the ground beside a tripod contraption. It was not as big as I was, but bigger than Bob. The officer said "Had that gone off last night it would have given you a headache."

The little corporal also had his twopenny's worth, "If it had gone off when you were near it this morning, it would have blown your head off."

Those brave men's words over the following years never went unheeded. From then on we took this war more seriously, it was no longer just a 'grown-ups' thing. Overnight we had grown up, we had passed through the barrier of fear, and from that time on, certainly for the remaining years of our childhood, nothing truly frightened us.

Mum took Anne and Jean looking for shops that might be open. There was no way of knowing how long the bombing campaign would last, if there were shops open, and if food was available. Now would be the best time to 'stock up' with rations available.

Jean recalls that Lipton's the grocers were open, despite the fact that fire had destroyed the upper floors; wooden beams were still smouldering as

Firemen and ARP Wardens search for survivors amid the still smouldering ruins of the city.

staff served customers as best they could with salvaged, usable stock. Butter at that time was sold by weight, and displayed in slabs, a customer's ration allowance would be cut off the slab. However the heat from the fires had all but melted it, and so the staff, with timbers on the upper floors smouldering above them, scooped butter with a spoon and wrapped it in greaseproof paper.

Later Mary and June, who were thirteen and fourteen years old at the time, were asked if they could help out at a field kitchen that had been set up for evacuated families, rescue personnel and so on. The girls set off about midday, Bob and I watched them as they stopped and chatted for a little while with the soldiers manning the road barricade.

The ground shook. A column of earth and smoke rose into the air at the very spot where my sisters would be. We ran to the barricade, the soldiers who seconds before had been flirting with them, forcibly stopped us as we attempted to run down the road. For the second time in the past twelve hours, time froze. To our relief we saw them emerging through the dust, a young soldier with his arm around Mary who was in deep shock. She was just staring straight ahead and she passed us without acknowledgement, just walking on.

June, 'the hero of the day', was visibly shaking. In her hands, which were protected by her green beret, was the largest piece of bomb shrapnel we ever saw, the size of a dinner plate and still much too hot to touch. Sobbing, tears running down her dust-covered face, she said "I threw Mary into the hedge and lay on top of her, this landed on the spot where seconds before we had stood."

Over the following years June became totally deaf in one ear, and shortly after that day, Mary started to have memory loss; today she has little or no recollection of her childhood, as the following chapters will bear witness. Personally I can think of nothing that would upset me more.

Four bombs had fallen near our house that night, one in a field over the road which left a large crater. Bob and I were joined by other children as we ran down one side then up the other. We collected shrapnel, incendiary bombs – both live and dead – and bomb fins. One boy had an aluminium case that had held the incendiaries, another claimed to have a shell nose cone.

The second bomb had fallen in the copse below our neighbour's house. It must have been the one that caused most of the damage to the back of our houses. The third bomb was the unexploded one, which would have caused the greatest damage had it exploded. The forth was the delayed action one down the road that went off as my sisters were passing.

We spent the afternoon clearing up the broken glass in the bedrooms, and then set about the cellar, cleaning and preparing for the strong possibility that there would be further raids to follow.

We had visitors, our neighbours, who suggested that they all share our shelter with us. Mum was all in favour, and it was understandable why. A young couple from the bungalow next door, together with Granny, Mr Evans and his wife – who both lived two doors down – brought their cat 'Tatee'. We all set to and made the cellar homely, the door was put back in place and reinforced with this and that, a settee and extra mattresses were put in place.

For the second night in succession the air raid sirens sounded. We were already in the shelter thirteen of us and one cat. Mrs Evans was talking to Tatee, "You will join the army when you grow up, Hitler will be sorry then. He understands every word I say, don't you my son"

Mr Evans had a baritone voice, and could often be heard singing in his garden. We suspected that he did so to deaden the sound of his wife talking to Tatee. The louder she shouted the louder he sang.

The bombing seemed to be further away, towards Devonport, and next morning the radio news broadcast announced that "A South Coast port last night received a second night of bombing, which was heavier than the previous night".

The night passed quickly, I slept through much of it. Over the past forty-eight hours I had been to school, looked for the King and Queen, shared fear, witnessed bravery, and acted stupidly. Sleep was an escape from reality, although I periodically woke to the sound of laughter, or of distant explosions. And while the sound of aircraft could be heard passing over, no bombs fell in our vicinity. When I finally awoke our guests had left, I was the only one awake, for us the last raid was over.

Dad made his way through the road block, saw us, stepped over the wall and gave each of us a hug in turn. Then we all went in, everyone speaking at once relating the events of the past days.

There would be no goodbyes, our school friends would never know where we had gone, and we in turn were left to wonder if they had survived the bombing unscathed. There was to be no continuity of friendships, just empty desks. Perhaps it was the best way, not knowing. And when the schools reopened after the raids it is highly likely that teachers were spared the trauma of calling the register, a new one would be compiled.

By four o'clock on the afternoon of 22 March 1941, we were ready to leave; furniture had been loaded into the removal van. Old faithful – the car which had been stored at Mumford's factory – was brought out, sheets, pillows, and blankets were loaded aboard.

This was going to be a long evening; firstly we would have to find a way out of Plymouth, and to add to our problems a light rain plus freshening winds had set in, the weather was deteriorating rapidly.

We were on our way to Cornwall.

Clearing up after the raids in Frankfort Street, Plymouth.

Chapter 4

A CORNISH HAVEN

Mum, who was just about 'all in', sat in the back of the car, a pillow under her head. The rest of us sat where we could be as comfortable as possible. Jean and I sat with Dad where extra pairs of eyes were going to be needed. Slowly in the failing light we skirted Plymouth, avoiding the worst of the destruction, and headed for Tavistock. Then leaving Devon behind we crossed the bridge over the River Tamar.

That night, unknown to me at the time, a very good friend of mine, who was then just six years old, walked with his mother in the rain and total darkness, away from the destruction of his home, north towards Tavistock, then on over the River Tamar to the relative safety of Cornwall, finding shelter in a chapel.

The misty rain was blowing almost horizontally, as we approached the edge of Dartmoor. Lights were blinkered due to blackout restrictions which didn't help. Our speed dropped to eighteen miles per hour or thereabouts. Dad was getting tired, he hadn't slept for twenty-four hours. He never told us how he managed to get from Truro to Plymouth, arriving early that morning.

On we motored, over the River Tamar into Cornwall, passing the Jamaica Inn on the moor towards Bodmin. The weather was getting worse, but at least Plymouth would get a rest tonight; aircraft could not fly in these weather conditions.

We pulled into the side of the road, the headlight shields were removed, there had to be more illumination law or no law, we just couldn't see the way ahead.

At Truro arrangements had been made to meet the John Julian removal van, and its crew who were to lead the way. Dad had yet to see the house that had been requisitioned for us at very short notice. We followed the blue van through narrow lanes and after a few miles we reached our new home. It was past midnight, and the worst was yet to come.

'Steep Holm' had recently been built, it stood on the side of a sloping site. From the roadside it looks like a bungalow, and from the estuary, a house – the front door being 'upstairs'.

We slowly followed the removal van down the drive which at that time was straight down from the gate to the front (or back, if you were viewing from the sea) door. It was pitch black, not a light could be seen, and we were heading straight into the full force of the wind and rain. Although we were less than fifty feet from the sea we couldn't see it; we imagined ourselves on the top of high cliffs with the raging Atlantic ocean below.

It was decided that due to the time of night, weather conditions and sheer exhaustion that we would unload the furniture and just leave it on the first floor – in the bedrooms, on the landing, anywhere. There were no lights; we were in total darkness. The van was backed up as close to the door as possible, on the lee side of the house, protected from the worst of the storm. Feeling our way in the dark, my silver cigarette lighter was put to good use as it produced just sufficient bursts of light to see.

There was only one way the piano could be taken into the house, which was through the French doors on the ground floor. This would entail loading it on to a small four-wheel bogey, wheeling it around the side of the house, and then halfway along the ground floor through the glass doors. The ground was just as the builders had left it, rough, and the piano was precariously balanced on the little trolley. Pulling, pushing, holding, Dad, three men and yours truly (dressed in short trousers, a shirt, and pullover) heaved, pushed and pulled, in the dark. In the howling wind and rain the piano tinkling a tune.

Eventually we arrived at the doors where Mum was waiting to open them. Disaster! The upstairs door had been opened, a gush of wind funnelled through the house, up the stairs, and the heavy French door slammed back, hitting mum on the arm which went through the glass, blood was everywhere!

Two pictures of the Pandora Inn, the top one taken in the 1920s, the lower probably taken in the 1950s.

Steep Holm – the 'front' door.

Steep Holm, now Harbour Lights, as it looks today.

There were no telephones at Restronguet point then, even if there had been we would never have found them, we didn't even know where we were. Dad had received medical training in the RAFVR. he applied a tourniquet out of torn sheets, as once again I held the lighter until the petrol ran out, my thumb was sore trying to relight it.

Mary and June made Mum comfortable, and I heard her say – and I reminded her of it many times over the following years, "I don't want to stay in this Godforsaken place, please take me to Burnham." (Two hundred miles away!).

Never had I slept as soundly as I did that night. I offer this advice to anyone reading this. If you ever find yourself in unfamiliar surroundings, in a blackout, hungry, wet and very tired, with a gale blowing outside, then take my advice, remove your wet clothes, wrap an eiderdown around yourself, throw pillows and bedding into an empty bath, then after replacing the plug to keep the spiders out – get in!

The view that greeted us the following morning has been instilled in my memory, where I hope it will remain always. The sun had risen over Carrick Roads to a calm sea which sparkled with light. The view stretched from St Antony light-house and the English Channel beyond, right through 180 degrees, along St Just in Roseland, then north to the River Fal where its wooded banks reached down to the water's edge.

Many species of sea birds bobbed on the surface of the water, diving under, then surfacing again, shaking their heads. A large tug was making her way up the channel.

Beyond Mylor Harbour out of sight lay Falmouth, where barrage balloons were slowly rising having been lowered in the storm. This would be our view for the next four-and-a-half years, our playground. We would familiarize ourselves with its ways, and its moods. In these waters we would fish, sail and salvage. However there would be more, much more, over the years to come. We would grow from children into teenagers, and there would be times when we would be called upon to act as adults and, I trust, responded accordingly. Here our characters would be moulded, by freedom, a close proximity to nature, and to war.

Carrick Roads was, and still is, an area of great natural beauty. The St Just in Roseland peninsula, now owned by the National Trust, together with the River Fal, looks exactly the same now as it did all those years ago when we lived there. To the west of Restronguet Point is a tidal creek known to us as Devoran Creek where a foot ferry ran across from the point to the Pandora Inn, on the Mylor side. The ferry was summoned by ringing a brass bell.

To the south and east there is a deep water harbour, known as Carrick Roads. To the north the deep waters of the River Fal wind their way up to Truro.

Large properties and their gardens now take up much of the area, where, in the period covered by this book, fields, shrubland, wooded areas and meadows dominated the landscape. There were five or six stone cottages plus two recently built houses and one bungalow, a retired railway carriage and, oh yes, a large steam yacht, moored just off the point. Mrs Job, the owner's wife

Falmouth Harbour from a watercolour painting dated 28 May 1940, annotated 'Norwegian Whalers, Dutch Liner and Dutch destroyers'.

Marble Head – home of Mr and Mrs Terry Blackburn. Probably taken in the late 1940s, the landing jetties at Tolverne can be seen centre background.

became a teacher at Feock school and their daughter Sonia shared many adventures with us.

Steep Holm stood in about four acres, the top two-thirds of which was planted with oats each year, together with the three- or four-acre field adjoining.

Mrs Blackburn and her four children, Ted, Terry, Violet and John lived at Marble Head Cottage. They had moved there from London to avoid the bombing. Mr Blackburn was in the army fighting in North Africa; he was later injured, discharged on medical grounds and returned to live with his family in 1944. Ted was a year younger than I was. Terry and Bob were both five years old at the time

Ted and his sister Vi, both of whom shared many adventures with us.

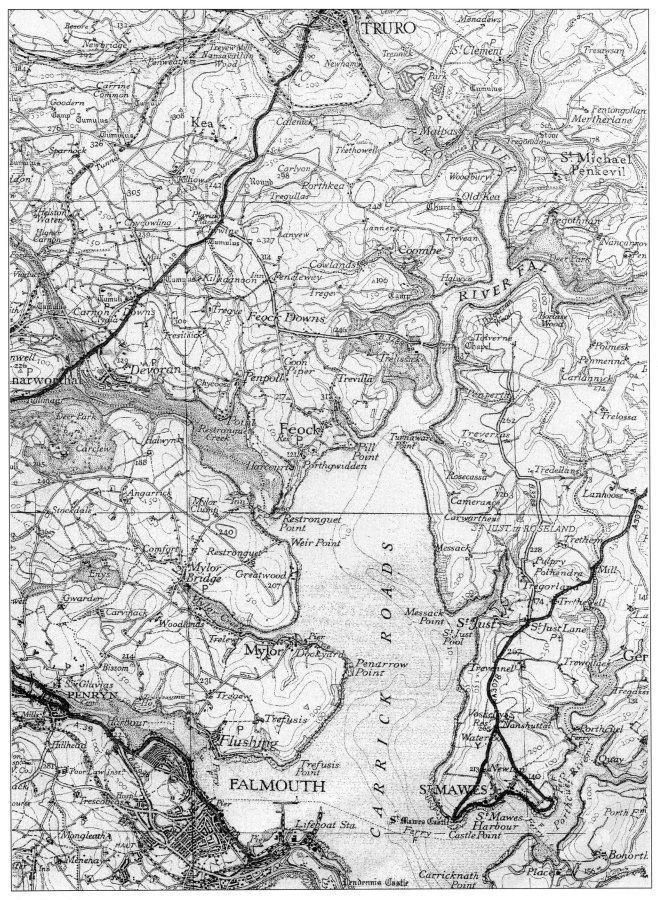

Our 'Patch'.

of our arrival, and we all became very good friends sharing many adventures, witnessing many unforgettable sights.

A carpenter and his sister, Mr and Miss Hartnett lived in the next cottage up the road, now called Seaways, unknowingly to either at the time, there was to be a combined Anglo-American night time operation undertaken on their behalf.

Mr Philipps, his wife and two sons, lived in the next house up the road. He was in appearance a double of Field Marshal Montgomery, a real character and a morale booster when things on the war front were at low ebb. Every morning he would walk up and down the aisle of the bus and shout, "Are we downhearted?"

We all had to respond with "No we are not!"

As the time of departure for the bus approached, Mr Philipps would take out his silver pocket watch, and dead on time would bang his cane on the floor. The driver had no option, the engine started we were off.

When the news from North Africa came that the 'Desert Rats' had Rommel on the run, there was such loud cheering that when a gentleman who was hard of hearing enquired the reason, he was informed by Mr Philipps that "the Germans in North Africa are in panic." The old chap replied in a loud voice, "Our'n will soon have them out of there!"

The man we called 'Monty's double' (a name given to the man who stood in for Monty as portrayed in the film) and my Father were good friends, one of their hobbies being, wine making, mead – honey wine – a speciality.

Mr Polglaze and his wife lived in a large house on the opposite side of the road to us; he was a retired chemist, a good engineer, a yachtsman, owning a 60-foot schooner, and, most importantly of all, he was a self self-sufficiency enthusiast.

On the eastern site of the point, from Laundry Cottage to Harcourt Farm, there were fields and a wooded area; the northern side was shrubland, where nothing grew except trees, gorse, and blackberry-covered hedges.

With the exception of a small holiday bungalow, Steep Holm was the only property on the eastern side; there was a footpath from the Point, along the Cliffside, to Looe Beach, used only by us, and the local rabbit catcher, Mr Evans, a dapper little man, always cheerful despite the fact that he was petrified of cats.

My sisters and I were enrolled at St Feock school, about a mile away. On our first day the two teachers were in a state of upheaval, evacuees had arrived almost overnight, class sizes doubled and there were not enough desks. Each pupil shared with another, chairs were urgently asked for in the village; we spent the morning of our first day, just settling in.

There were Bristolians, Devonians, Channel Islanders, Londoners, and last but not least, Cornish. All were in a state of bewilderment.

Shortly after our arrival, I had to sit the second part of the Scholarship examination. It would be easy to make excuses, other than the simple truth, which was, I fluffed it. I just sat there in a daydream.. Maths was no problem, it was the rest of it that flummoxed me, including writing an essay on 'a day in the life of a farmer.' Before our arrival in Cornwall I had only seen a cow from a distance; how could I write an essay on a farm hand, sitting on a three-legged stool, milking a cow?

If I had a problem – and I did – give a thought for others taking the same exam who, had recently left large cities, and had never seen a farm. Ted once told me that he couldn't wait to be evacuated from London as he wanted to see a cow. Most of my friends, who ended up going to grammar school, were from farming families.

And so ended my dreams of being a sea captain; the Headmaster at Two Mile Hill School might have had a point when he recorded, "Harding will only go down in history if he shoots the Prime Minister." In my defence, it was a new school, I had just been through a blitz or two and, to cap it all, I was at that time being bullied.

Why the bully picked on me, a newcomer to his life, without any justifiable reason I just can't say; but pick on me he did.

Paul was his name, slightly taller than I was, plump but not fat, and he wore a blue school cap which covered his red hair. Most children at that time wore hand-me-down clothes, that didn't always fit. Not Paul he was always smartly dressed.

He made my life a misery from the first day, always pushing, tripping me up, challenging me to a fight after school, "Johnny short legs" he called me, this bully from Bristol. I didn't know at that time, there being no way of doing so, but if anyone person in my life unwittingly did me a good turn it was Paul. I was not happy at Feock School; I was on the road to nowhere.

The 'final-straw' moment arrived; it was play time and I was showing Reg James my lighter when a hand from behind snatched it from me, and over the wall it went into the vicarage garden. The bully's nose was inches from mine, "If you want it go and find it."

I remember the silence as my new-found friends waited, watching my reaction. I punched him with all the power I could muster. He just stood there with a look of utter surprise on his face, and I hit him again,

This time he staggered back, and a shout went up "Fight! Fight!" A ring of chanting spectators and two brawling boys slowly moved down the playground towards the school building.

Paul wanted out; I was having none of it. Adrenalin was running high, and I had the upper hand. Miss Williams, the head teacher grabbed me by the ear and then, still holding it, literally frog-marched me down the steps into the classroom. St Feock School and I ended our short and unhappy association. The lighter was found, after my friends and I spent most of Saturday morning searching for it.

Not long after 'the fight' Paul, accompanied by his father, arrived at our house; he was going back to Bristol. We shook hands, despite a few bruises there were no hard feelings. Dad bought Paul's bicycle for me, for two pounds. I became the owner of the finest bicycle I had ever seen, on which, I'd often ride to my new school six miles away

Truro Senior Boys School and I began our happy association. Mr Delahunt, the head master, was a strict disciplinarian without resorting to physical punishment. The school had previously been a Technical College and was still referred to as 'The Tec'. It still had equipment used in its previous life which was put to good use by first class teachers. Here I would restart my interrupted education with renewed vigour.

My teacher, Mr Rowe, had written and had published science books. He was a quiet-natured man, never raising his voice, he didn't need to as his every word was listened to and absorbed. Under his guidance one pupil passed the entrance

Truro Senior Boy's School. Now the City Library.

exam for Dartmouth Naval College, another became a flight engineer for BOAC – and later a commercial airline pilot. There were several successful, businessmen who owed much of their success to Mr Rowe, and yours truly – not the brightest by a long chalk, having left school at fourteen years of age. I found myself four and a half years later at Signals Intelligence, Bletchley Park under the watchful eye of Winston Churchill.

I was hooked on science from day one at school, from the magnetism stage, right through to the radio receivers. With the help of Mr Polglaze and his engineering workshop, plus Mr Hartnell providing wooden bases, all manner of electrical gadgets were turned out. I was the plague of Farm Industries Truro, scrounging magnets from tractor magnetos, copper wire, and nuts and bolts; anything and everything was put to good use. As we will see later nothing would keep me away from school.

I was called to Mr Delahunt's office and questioned about various aspects of my life: "My father's occupation? I don't know sir." An answer I had been told to give, if anyone asked – careless talk and all that. "The blitz?" he continued.

"We were very lucky sir", a pause, looking up at me standing there, then back to his notes.

"Arrangements have been made for certain pupils to retake the scholarship exam," he said. "Would you like your name put forward?" My answer was instant, absolutely no hesitation, "No thank you sir." I was happy there, at Truro Senior Boys' School. Never in my life have I ever regretted my spontaneous decision. In one week's time I would be the school hero, and it came from an unlikely source, sport.

Shoes were strictly rationed, clothing coupons, were issued to each individual, one pair on average per year. Of course there was some juggling in families, those in need, jumped the queue. And as we grew out of clothing, it was handed down. However not all pupils came from large families, and so for that reason, anyone picked to play soccer had to have football boots.

The local boys, had an advantage over those from the cities, the reason was this: a boy evacuated from a bombed city would be able to take with him only the bare necessities, football boots were not on the list. A pity, as it is highly likely that these lads had kicked tin cans around in back alleys and were very good players. But rules were rules, no boots no game.

I had never played football, or seen it played; there being no television then, and as for rules, "what rules?" But I owned a pair of football boots, sent to me by a distant cousin, who obviously had never seen me, as they were three or, perhaps even four sizes too big.

If anyone reading this book is lucky enough to spend a holiday in Cornwall, and while there you are enjoying a quite drink in a local pub, you might just happen to spot an elderly gentleman sitting in a corner smiling. There could even be a soft chuckle, and a shaking of his beer gut. Do yourself a favour, listen to his Cornish dialect. He might, if you refill his glass a time or two, recall, the Schools Cup Final, in May 1941.

The sport's master stood in front of the class, "We desperately need one more player for the final, have I volunteer, someone who owns a pair of football boots?" I was as shocked as anyone when my hand went up, this new boy, this titch, "That does it!"

Paper, the *Daily Mirror* strip cartoons of Jane and all, went into the toe and heels of those boots; two or perhaps even three pairs of socks were pulled on, and I was ready.

There was no shortage of support, ignoring shouts of "Look at Harding, he looks like Donald Duck. He's only playing because he's got boots." I couldn't have agreed more, I felt like Donald Duck.

In the first half I didn't kick the ball once. I ran after it but by the time I got to where it was, it wasn't. However two goals each was not bad, despite the fact that I stopped playing for a few minutes to watch a train pulling out of Truro station, and a fellow team mate explained that trains never went up steep hills. I didn't know that, but that train was a sight I can tell you – power, steam, black smoke. Where was I? Oh yes, football.

The game, thank goodness, was nearing the end. My ankles were sore, I did kick the ball twice, to shouts of "Oh well played Harding!"

If you don't believe me, then ask the gentleman in the corner at the local, this is what happened. No further score, the opposing team in matching shirts and shorts, 2, our team, 2. The ball stopped dead in its tracks, between the opposition's goal posts and me. I couldn't miss, allow me write what happened next in slow motion.

Footballs were made of thick leather, heavy when wet. They had a rubber bladder held in place with a boot lace; I know, I saw it there on the ground four feet away. Never have I put so much force into my right leg, two-and-a-bit steps, kick through the air it went high up, straight between the goal posts. The goalie looked up, then ran like hell, his arm over his head, the heavy ball wasn't the reason for him taking evasive action, no, the ball hadn't moved, I had missed, my right boot had come off, and was heading straight for him.

Action on my part didn't cause the mayhem that followed, I was an innocent bystander. One boot on, the other behind the goal posts; an opportunist in our team ran up and kicked the ball between the vacated goal posts, not me. I have to say it was hardly cricket, taking advantage like that.

Bedlam broke out, rules, made up on the spot, were quoted, the referee just would not stop blowing his whistle. The losing team might have had matching shirts and shorts, but they were miners' sons from Camborne, weaned on fresh air and pasties, and they were heading straight for me. Why me? I only kicked the ball twice.

There followed, what I can only describe as a light-hearted cross between a wrestling contest and a rugby scrum. Boys present who had no football boots joined in, I enjoyed the scrap more than the football.

It cannot be learned, or copied. Those of us who have it, never lose it; my school pals were past masters at the art of laughing at themselves. We had won the football match but lost the scrap.

Other boys from Feock School arrived at Truro Senior Boys'. Reggie James, Teddy Blackburn were two of my friends; we travelled together on the bus, also spent time together at midday.

Our parents had to pay both for bus fares and meals. Each day we were given one shilling, spending seven pence on the bus fair and a half-penny for milk, which left four pence halfpenny for a midday snack. In fine weather we would ride our bicycles to Playing Place, leave our bikes in the garage, then catch the bus from Falmouth, or on occasions ride the full distance of five miles each way. This became the norm as we grew older as saving the bus fare gave us a wider choice of lunch. Also, not having to wait and hour after school for the bus we were home earlier. As we will see, the saved time was put to very good use.

During the war the Ministry of Food set up a string of restaurants throughout the country, which gave workers an off-ration hot meal. Please don't take my judgment of 'British Restaurants' – as they were known – as the norm, but for what it's worth my assessment was 'one notch above the workhouse, three notches below a GWR station cafe'.

A bowl of red-looking luke-warm soup, probably made with Knorr cubes, was tuppence half-penny, which left us tuppence; one penny for a hot drink and one penny for three bread rolls purchased from a bakery at the end of Cathedral Lane, just around the corner.

We would sneak the rolls into the restaurant under our pullovers, buy the 'soup' and dip the bread in it.

Things have not changed over the years since, they were, and are, a special breed of their own – 'officials' who are full of their own importance. This one was in all probability an ex-army sergeant major, sporting a twisted moustache, shouted with a very loud voice, just inches away from my ear "Food is not to be brought into this establish-

ment." And to cap it all we were marched out, leaving a bowl of red-looking liquid on the table.

But we took it in our stride, the soup was probably made from scraps left on plates the day before, and we had three bread rolls one day and the very best Cornish pasties the next, bought from the same shop in Cathedral Lane. I mention this because of a memory I have regarding a stranger's kindness.

We were standing in the queue next to her – three of us – and I can only assume that she must have overheard our conversation as to our lunch – three bread rolls. In no way were we complaining, as a matter of fact we liked the rolls, fresh from the oven. Despite our protests and assurances that we were not hungry, all three of us were taken to a nearby hotel and for the first time in our lives, in 'posh' surroundings, we were waited on. I cannot remember the menu, or the meal, I was overawed by the sheer grandeur of my surroundings and gratitude for the generosity we had received.

When the sailing barges Mary or Shamrock were alongside Truro Quay unloading their cargo of road stone, we would buy our lunch and hurry down, sometimes sitting on a bollard just watching. On the deck a 'donkey' stationary engine would lift large wicker baskets full of stone, out from the hold. Then the contents would be tipped into a lorry. This unloading operation went like clockwork; firstly the basket was lowered into the hold, where two men with shovels filled it, next the winch man, usually the skipper of the vessel, wrapped a pulling rope three times around a shining capstan. Taking up the strain, this lifted the basket and its contents up via a pulley on the end of the ship's boom, which in turn, depending on the lay of the vessel, would be pulled towards the chap standing on the lorry. This was tipped by him and the whole procedure repeated. Two baskets were used, one being loaded, the second being tipped.

On top of the hard-working little engine was a cooling tank, which boiled, vibration causing the water, probably sea water, to spill over on to the cylinder block, which was red with rust. Steam rose from the cooling block. The vertical exhaust pipe had no silencer and when under strain it gave a deep hollow sound. When the empty basket was

Truro as it looked during the author's youth.

Sailing barges sit alongside the quay in Truro.

being lowered the sound quickened, smoke rings drifted slowly up before dispersing.

We were, as you have no doubt gathered, in love with those sturdy hard-working little ships.

The lorry loaded, time for a quick cuppa, and lunch; down below in the fo'c'sle, a copper kettle steaming on an iron stove, tea in an enamel mug stained with use, mahogany-panelled bulkheads, a brass gimbled oil lamp next to a barometer hanging on the mast pillar, and the smell of pipe tobacco filling the air.

These coastal sailing barges were at the end of their era and I feel privileged to have such memories. But it was war time and, despite many requests for a trip along the Cornish coast during school holidays, we were always politely turned down. In the relative tranquillity, tied up alongside Truro Quay, it was a different ball game to the English Channel in war time.

Every schoolboy was given the opportunity to volunteer for up to ten days per year, helping out on local farms. Each would be given a blue card, stamped by the teacher, recording time off. Farmers requiring helpers would stand in front of the class and ask for a given number of helpers. Payments, lunch etc. were all read out in front of the teacher, and questions asked, and answered.

Old hands knew the ropes, good farmers and those best avoided, good lunches and so on. "Go with Brown," was the advice from boys who had used up their year's quota. And so, as the class had a relief lady teacher, history and all that, for the first and only time I volunteered.

Two of the 'old hands' jumped into the cab of the Bedford Lorry. I was soon to find out why. Mr Brown had only one eye and, in my opinion, very little sensation in his right foot. The accelerator was either flat on the cab floor, or off the pedal. Adding to that he drove in straight lines, and those in the back, which included myself, were thrown, first to the front and then to the back, piling on top of one and another. No wonder he drove so fast, if he hadn't a few of us would have jumped out and walked back to school. It was that dangerous!

On we sped through country lanes, then farm tracks until we arrived at the farm. After a cold drink and buttered bread we were put to work, picking up potatoes. Working in pairs we had a

section to cover, marked with empty sacks at each end. It wasn't hard work, a little back-breaking perhaps, however as I didn't have far to stoop to reach the potatoes all went well until we noticed that we were always the last to finish and the pair next to us always finished first. They were the 'old hands' at this game, we were greenhorns, and let's face it, slow on the uptake. The marker bags had been moved, our stretch was much longer than theirs. But they were not the only 'old hands' on that field, that day.

Mrs Brown was lovely, a Cornish Megs Jenkins (a famous film star at that time), sitting in a large farm kitchen. We had chicken soup, with thick slices of homemade bread, washed down with fresh milk.

At four o'clock as per regulations, we finished. I have already said, Mr Brown had only one eye and he was driving the tractor, but his sight was good enough to watch the 'old hands'. So when it came to wages time Eddie (my partner and I) had one shilling and sixpence extra in wages than the 'old hands'. When they protested they were told, "These two lads picked up five bags more than you." And to add salt in their wounds we sat in the cab going home.

All in all a very enjoyable day. I was rich, five shillings and six pence rich; I slept with my newly gained fortune under my pillow and counted it over and over again. I gave Mum three shillings and sixpence towards new shoes, which cost four shillings and eleven pence, plus coupons of course. I never volunteered for farm work again; I wish now, that I had kept my blue card.

Dad joined the river patrol, in preference to the Home Guard. The area of the River Fal above the King Harry ferry was covered at night by his craft, an ex River Thames private motor launch. The adjoining area from King Harry down to Falmouth was the responsibility the Royal Navy, using a much larger and more powerful vessel. Dad often said that the two nights spent on the water helped him to unwind from the pressures of his 'day job' with the Air Ministry.

I often met Dad from the evening bus, walking home with him down the hill from Harcourt. Not only did this give us a chance to have a chat, I got first look at the 'Knockout' comic. I knew he had been disappointed at my not passing the Eleven

This photograph of the River Patrol was taken before Dad joined.

Plus exam, he was not aware of the second chance that I had turned down.

News on the war front was not good, it was England's darkest hour, and so I was pleasantly surprised to see him smiling. "I've bought a boat," he said, "a rowing boat, you'll love her. There are fish to be caught out there in the estuary, we will get a net, and help ourselves, I'll need your support." His pace quickened as his excitement and enthusiasm took over, "First a herring net, then a trammel."

I liked the idea of a boat; however the rest of it was new to me. The U-boat threat was at its height, essential food supplies were at risk. Dad continued "We must look at ways of providing as much food from the land and the sea as possible."

That was it, from the time it had taken to walk from Harcourt down the hill to our gate, a seed had been sown, and that seed grew, and plans were turned into action, neighbours became willing partners, each with their own contributions and speciality. Overnight, residents living at Restronguet Point and beyond became fishermen, farmers, beekeepers, and rabbit catchers. We were light years ahead of today's environmentalists, and we had to be. There was no plastic then, no dustmen called, we were self sufficient in water supplies, and used the bare minimum of electricity. There were no refrigerators, television sets, or washing machines, no telephones, central heating, or National Health Service. In war time, everyone pulled together, the strong helping the weak.

The boat had to be brought down the Fal. Dad, leaving at high water had the ebbing tide in his favour. We were excited, waiting in anticipation in what would have, and should have been, a happy occasion for us all. We stood on the shore, as he approached.

Everyone alive at that time remembers where they were when war was declared. I am positive that every school boy remembers where they were, when the news broke that the German battle-cruiser *Bismarck* had sunk the *Hood*. Even now, over sixty five years later as I type these words, I recall the heartache I felt then.

St Feock Home Guard. Shortly after this photograph was taken, my friend Charles Gilbert joined, on his sixteenth birthday.

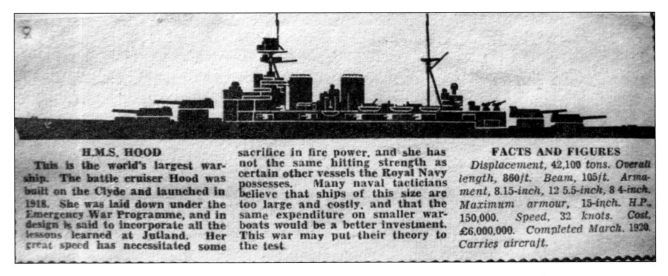

H.M.S. HOOD

This is the world's largest warship. The battle cruiser Hood was built on the Clyde and launched in 1918. She was laid down under the Emergency War Programme, and in design is said to incorporate all the lessons learned at Jutland. Her great speed has necessitated some sacrifice in fire power, and she has not the same hitting strength as certain other vessels the Royal Navy possesses. Many naval tacticians believe that ships of this size are too large and costly, and that the same expenditure on smaller warboats would be a better investment. This war may put their theory to the test.

FACTS AND FIGURES

Displacement, 42,100 tons. Overall length, 860ft. Beam, 105ft. Armament, 8 15-inch, 12 5.5-inch, 8 4-inch. Maximum armour, 15-inch. H.P., 150,000. Speed, 32 knots. Cost, £6,000,000. Completed March, 1920. Carries aircraft.

A contemporary newspaper clipping which provides some fateful facts regarding HMS Hood.

Dad's actions and the look on his face as he brought our new boat into the shore, said it all. There were no smiles, our waves were not returned. He didn't look at us, just stepping on to the shore and looking out over the water he said, "The *Hood* has been lost, there are very few survivors."

My grief was silent, just tears and an urgent desire to swallow. My first close-up view of our beautiful little boat was distorted through watery eyes.

Our boat was called *Swordfish*, named by a previous owner. It is said that to change a ship's name is unlucky, and so *Swordfish* she was, and *Swordfish* she remained. Clinker built (over-lapping planks) she was fifteen feet long, pointed at each end, lightly constructed of pine, with ash ribs. Norway was probably her country of origin, she had been in her past life a ship's boat. Large bronze rings, used to hoist her on board her parent vessel, were still in place, fore and aft.

There was only one rowing position, amidships.

The large pair of oars would require practice; at first it took two of us, one oar each, to propel her through the water.

This little craft would soon become the nucleus of our lives. In her we would become the Huckleberry Finns of the Fal. If it happened, we were there, and if we were there, it happened.

Painted green down to the waterline, and tarred below, in the winter months we would dry her off, turn her upside-down then tar her bottom. The hot tar would 'run' down each year on to the green paint, and to cover it we tarred it, and so each year she became one green plank less, one black plank more.

We, my brother sisters, and friends, loved every inch of her, from her wide gunnels, to her ribs, which became smooth and shiny, rubbed by bare feet. Like all boats, large and small, she had a soul. If only we had a photograph. It's always 'if only' when looking back. But cameras were forbidden on tidal waters during the war years. Aboard her, as children, we would, fish, swim, and picnic. Later as we grew older, she would be put to more serious uses.

Chapter 5

AFLOAT

During the summer holidays in 1941, one of our favourite pastimes would be to load the *Swordfish* with victuals, including potatoes, parsnips, onions, and obtainable soup ingredients. A large tin was used for a cooking pot. Complete with a loaf of bread – which was about to become rationed – off we would go along the shore, pull in on a beach, light a fire, place the tin on it into which sea water had been added, then add the ingredients. When ready we would sit around dipping large chunks of bread into the pot, and with charcoal-covered cheeks mutter such things as 'super', 'whizzo' along with any other RAF slang words of the day. In truth, the flavour was nothing of the sort; it was the adventure, plus our surroundings that gave it just that little something special.

As always on days like these, one memory stands out above the rest. We had landed on the beach under Trelissick House, Ted and Terry, my brother and sisters Anne and Jean, the usual six of us. The *Swordfish* was lying just offshore, moored with an anchor stuck into the sand. No sooner had we stepped ashore, than the law of 'owner's rights' raised its head. The item in dispute was a sailor's hat, complete with its HMS silk ribbon, a beachcombers dream at that time. The two parties in dispute were Terry and Bob,

"I saw if first," sez Terry.

"I bagged it," sez Bob.

"I've got it," sez Terry, plonking the still wet hat on his head, then running off along the beach. Now, if ever you spot a cat digging up plants in your garden take a leaf out of Bob's book, grab a parsnip by the pointed end, bring it back over your shoulder and throw, as if throwing a knife at a tree. It's the most accurate missile known to man, or in this case boy. End over end it went, straight as a die, hitting Terry between his shoulders.

I would like to record that it knocked the hat off, but it just hit the back of a fast-moving boy. Ted took his brother's side, I took Bob's, and in no time at all, we had run out of vegetable missiles,

and we had to revert to using stones, and driftwood.

Now Ted was a year younger than I was, but he was taller and well built. Not that I was a coward, but I had my brother and sisters to consider, so a strategic withdrawal took place.

We high-tailed it to the boat, grabbing the anchor and throwing it on board. Pushing and paddling at the same time we were soon out of range. Terry still had the hat and was waving it in the air, but both he and his brother were bare footed, and they had to walk home.

Just out of range we slowly rowed, as they walked along the rocky shore, slipping on the seaweed-covered rocks. Residents living at Pill Creek were serenaded that with 'What shall we do with the drunken sailor', or at least the words we knew. As always, the next morning as we were eating our breakfast, the door opened, two chairs were dragged up to the table, and helping themselves to whatever was going, with no mention of the previous day from the winners or losers – "What shall we do today?"

The first fishing net arrived in time for the summer holidays of 1941; it was a herring net useful for catching many different species of fish. It was about 25 or 30 yards long with corks at the top edge and lead weights at the bottom. It was 'set' at right angles to the shore, and held in place at the beach end by a rope tied to a rock, the other by an anchor.

We 'set' the net from the stern of the *Swordfish* after tea, then as late in the evening as possible gave it the once over, removing any fish before the crabs and cormorants ended up with more than their fair share.

As I have said, being on tidal waters after dark was forbidden, as naval patrol boats were always on the lookout for offenders. All sorts of penalties were in force, which ranged from going up before the beak, who could order the confiscation of boat and gear, to a large fine, or a spell inside at His

Majesties' Pleasure. Or if the judge took a dislike to you, all the lot. There is in Mylor churchyard a gravestone which marks the end of one poor seaman, caught on the water after dark and shot dead with a musket. I should add this tragic event took place a long time ago.

There was another risk for us. Dad was the engineer on the River Fal section of the area patrolled, and it would have been embarrassing for him if we were caught to say the least. The fact that he knew was neither here nor there, but we were never caught as such. Once we were unknowingly showing a light and, answering a knock at the door, found half the Royal Navy standing outside; two had rifles on their shoulders!

One night I was alone 'running' along the net, removing the odd fish, one ear listening for the sound of an engine, when, I heard the sound of voices, very near. Whoever it was, they were drifting, allowing the tide to take them along the shore. I took off my shorts and pullover and in my 'birthday suit' quietly slipped over the side into the water, and swam ashore. I have often wondered, did they know I was there?

We nearly always had a surplus of fish. The net was set according to demand, on average I'd say three times per week: mackerel, the odd sea bass, and scads – my favourite, although not over popular with the locals. Later, when we had a trammel net, we caught pollack, and even the odd salmon peel.

Mr Harnett made us a cart which was taken around the local area, usually by Anne, who sold fresh fish for one penny each. I can never remember one single day when she returned with unsold fish. On occasions, in the summer months, we would have heavy catches, and then we would take the boat to Looe Beach, walk around the village, informing every one that fish were to be had right on their doorstep.

The net and its operation, putting out and bringing in, cleaning out the seaweed, loading and unloading it from the boat and so on, was, our 'pigeon' so to speak. It was time-consuming but time in the summer months – with double summer time – was something we had plenty of, and Dad hadn't. However, he loved the water and being on it.

Our boating companion, Mark Taylor.

A very good friend of Dad's, Mr Visick, had a son-in-law, Mark Taylor, who was a marine engineer in the Merchant Navy. Mark loved the boat and all that went with it, and we liked him and all that went with him. Everything we learnt about boats, he taught us; together we made a lug sail, and we had a mast given to us by a friend, a retired sea captain. The sail was made from barrage balloon material, found on the shore after breaking adrift in a gale as they often did. They were made of silk (plastic was unheard of at that time), light and strong, silver in colour. There was no hiding the source, everyone knew where it originated, but who could say anything. Farmers covered hayricks with it, boat owners their boats, it became the war time tarpaulin. If 'it' needed protecting from the weather, we covered 'it' with barrage balloon material.

Mark being older than us, and younger than Dad, was a go-between, often explaining Dad's point of view to us, and vice versa, never once taking sides.

I had a three-foot-six-inch Gentleman's pond yacht that was in need of some loving tender care, but despite this she would sail like a witch. Bob, Mark and I would take her well out into the estuary, point its bow towards home and would race her, and when the wind and sea conditions were in her favour; she gave us a run for our money.

The tender loving care required was mostly cosmetic; she had been stowed away for some time, moths had got at the sails here and there, but nothing serious. Her stays and running gear were slightly worse for wear and so on, and Mark took her away to "see what could be done".

Mum shouted up the stairs, "Are you awake John?" I was. "Put your slippers on and come down son, we have something to show you."

Mark's wife, who sadly passed away recently aged ninety-two, recalled that evening the last time I spoke with her on the telephone, me entering the dining room, half asleep, just staring at the sight before me. Half reaching out to touch, almost afraid to do so, the yacht's hull had been re-varnished, its tall mast repaired, the steering gear had been reconditioned but all its originality had been retained, standing on the table with her mast almost touching the ceiling. I was speechless, not only at the sight before my eyes, but at the love that had been put into the workmanship. Mark stood with his young wife, both with a look of pride. I just didn't know how to thank them enough. Leaving the room I paused, and smiled at Mark; I never saw him again.

The yacht stood on her new stand in the hall, and every time I passed by her I would run my fingers over her beautiful lines, and remember, with fondness and sadness.

It was wartime; thousands of children had to come to terms with grief, there being no counselling then. I stared at the ceiling at night, fantasising that Mark and his shipmates were adrift in a boat, and perhaps had found an island where they lived a Robinson Crusoe life. But as dawn broke reality returned, and I remembered once again Dad's conversation with Mr Polglaze on the day we had first heard the news.

"The Sea all around an oil tanker catches fire, some survivors have been known to escape by swimming under the water surfacing briefly, pushing the burning oil clear, taking a deep breath, and diving under again." Over and over these words echoed in my mind, the hurt would not go away, until it was decided that our model

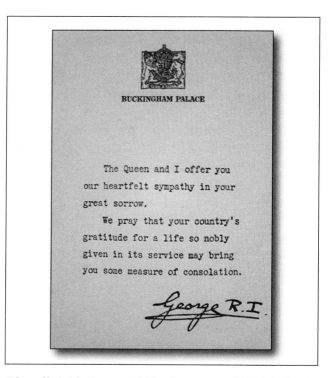
The official letter sent following news of Mark's death.

boat, Mark's and mine, would be placed in store, spending the remaining war years in Mr Polglaze's garage.

Let's pause for a while and give thought for children who had to come to terms with grief, the loss of their father or brother perhaps. Sadly it happens in war and peace time too, but during the period covered by this book there was the 'not knowing' aspect that must have been the hardest to come to terms with. 'Missing in Action' must have brought unbearable pain, and endless prayers to many who suffered loss.

Sitting in the classroom one day, I raised my hand, which meant a trip to the toilet. As I walked across the playground Mr Delahunt was slowly walking back and forth his hand around the shoulder of a pupil who was looking at the ground, thinking of his brother who was in the RAF and missing. The headmaster chose the playground for occasions like this, away from the headmaster-and-pupil atmosphere of his office.

As I have said it was the country's 'darkest hour', 1941. The Battle of Britain was being fought in the air, the Battle of the Atlantic was at its height, and not at that time going too well. Ships carrying supplies and food were being sunk by U-boats not only on the open seas, but right on our doorstep.

Throughout England the 'Dig for Victory' campaign was in full swing. Farmers were given incentives to plough up grassland, The Prime Minister, Winston Churchill said at that time, "The whole of the warring nations are engaged, not only soldiers, but the entire population; men, women and children."

On Restronguet Point the call to produce more home-grown food was answered. With the exception of a very small paddock near the ferry, all fields and the top two-thirds of our garden were 'put under the plough'.

Children also played their part. The first step was to be as self-sufficient as possible in food production. Dad drove a very small Ransome tractor home from Truro. It ran on tracks and had a top speed of about two miles per hour. He set about ploughing up the area of our garden not dedicated to more professional use such as growing cereals, and any other garden in the area with access for the tractor.

In the following years anything that grew underground such as potatoes, carrots, onions, and the such-like grew well. However, we and our neighbours had one problem: rabbits, lots and lots of them. And they in turn had their problem, skins were in demand, and the rest of them tasted good, roasted, or in a stew.

We tried shooting them with the airgun, throwing stones, and putting wire netting around the vegetable patch, all to no avail. The only answer was catching them – my department – the answer being wire nooses at a shilling a dozen.

My problem was I could catch them and kill them, I even learnt how to gut them, but skin them? No Sir! Not me. My customers, of which there was no shortage, had to buy them at sixpence each, skin them and sell the skins, take it or leave it. But Brian Ferris who lived at Harcourt had an eye for business, he would skin them for a penny and sell the skins.

Most of our neighbours kept chickens and so we followed suite. Theirs were in large runs, ours ran free, laying their eggs in hedges or long grass, even once on the beach. It was a game of hide and seek; they would hide the whereabouts of their nest and its contents, we would spend ages watching their every movement in order to find it. Chickens had one natural disadvantage, when laying an egg;

they would cackle their heads off, which at first, gave the game away but they soon became wise to little humans 'waiting for the call', and so these little feathered cheats would lay the egg, quietly strut off well clear, then cackle like mad. A while later they'd turn up with baby chicks in tow, and we ended up with more chicks, more hens, and more eggs.

Dad decided also to keep bees, and bought two hives, their contents and equipment. As far as I am aware he had no previous experience in hive management, but all credit to him, soon our house became the meeting place of bee-keepers from a wide area. Mum was all for it, bee-keepers were entitled to a sugar allowance, and Mum took two or even three spoonfuls in her tea. The honey produced after the first year was so encouraging that it was decided to expand, overseas, to Restronguet Mylor.

A deal had been made between the two parties. Dad would install a hive full of bees, the owner of a large garden and orchard would – in return – have his apple trees pollinated, and the odd jar or two of honey; deal done. However the hive and its inhabitants, would have to be transported by rowing boat, which involved a nervous, reluctant, assistant, me.

The hive was carried down the bank, across the slippery seaweed, then placed into the stern of the *Swordfish*. I rowed while Dad puffed smoke into the hive at the taking off and landing ramp to calm them down. All went well until we landed on the beach. I took one end of the hive Dad the other, resting it on the boat's gunnels. Then both of us climbed over the side, giving a little more smoke all around, and once again we each took a side of the hive, Dad walking backwards towards the shore. I can't say where the bee or bees came from, our hive perhaps, or a local colony defending their territory. One or two went up the leg of Dad's shorts, and by the look on his face must have stung him. He panicked, dropped his end into the water and it topped over on to its back, but miraculously the bees seemed unperturbed by their ordeal.

Dad's reputation of being a bee-keeper spread throughout the area. One day he was asked to remove a swarm of bees from the local chapel, which, we believe, didn't go exactly to plan but the operation became one of those taboo subjects! Dad's face was swollen from stings, and Anne had seen him on his bicycle peddling like mad with a thousand or two bees following. If Mum thought that questions were going to be asked, she would stare at us, with a finger to her lips and shake her head.

In many ways Restronguet was similar to an island community, living in close proximity with neighbours a bond develops that is hard to define. Framed by the surrounding water, protected in isolation, brings inhabitants closer, without intrusion, which is just the way it should be. However, the period covered in this book was far from normal, there was a very real possibility that the Battle of the Atlantic would be lost, when surrender or starvation could be the only option.

As children we had an inkling of the seriousness facing us, despite attempts to shield us from reality. We accepted grown-ups' judgments and guidance most of the time without question. Parents took food production to heart, fresh vegetables, fish and eggs, but in our view they took things a little too far at times.

Boiled stinging nettles "full of vitamins and iron", they said, but it wasn't the good things in it that bothered me, it was the caterpillars. I was force-fed the green slimy stuff, Mum holding my nose tight, and when I gasped for breath in would go spoonfuls. I held it in the side of my mouth, urged if it got near to my throat, sometimes accidentally-on-purpose knocking the plate off the table. If you want my honest opinion, boiled stinging nettles were not good for me.

The thing that puzzled me was why Mary or June didn't require vitamins and iron, or Mum and Dad for that matter. If stinging nettles weren't bad enough, how about this one: "Frumerity" Dad called it. He'd always had it for breakfast when he lived on the island of Steep Holm he said. No wonder he left.

It's my view that he made up the name and the recipe! Take a stone jar, fill one-third of the jar with washed wheat, and add one part-water, one-part milk until the jar is full. If there is a war on make that four-parts water one-part watered-down milk. Leave standing overnight in a Cornish range.

It tastes like ground up bicycle tyre inner tubes, cooked in cats wee. "Why don't you feed the wheat to the chickens, and eat the eggs?" I

pleaded as I chewed and chewed. "Eat it up its good for you, don't you know there's a war on!"

I hated stinging nettles, full stop. I was once caught using a swearword "sod it". Gasps of horror all round. I knew the ropes, marched up the drive behind the garage where the healthiest stinging nettles grew, shorts and pants down around my ankles, usual clap-trap, "this is going to hurt me more than it hurts you," then, nettles held in a gloved hand, swish 'two for the price of one'.

Two fields away from our house, at the side of a wooded area, was an apple orchard, about half an acre in size. Access was easy for us, along the beach, over the rocks, heads down out of sight; a game, a commando raid. Bob once even wore his tin hat!

Up the bank hidden by trees, in less than a minute we were off back home the way we had come, each carrying a bag of windfalls. Each raid was meticulously planned in advance, manoeuvres carried out. We even sent Anne, Jean and Violet out in the boat dressed as boys, as a decoy. We blackened our faces and camouflaged our clothes with all manner of flora.

The memories of the raids lingered longer than the taste of apple pie, dumplings, or stewed apple and custard. Dad loved apple dumplings, always he gave us a history lesson when eating this favourite: "King Henry the Eighth could never understand how the apple got into the dumpling you know," he would smile. "If Mum had made the pastry for His Highness's dumpling, the mystery would not be, how did the apple get in, but how do you get it out."?

The groundsman who cared for the orchard looked a nice enough chap, friendly, always laughing, it was his dogs who caused the problem. They knew we were pinching apples, we knew they knew we were pinching apples. They would sniff at us when we delivered fish, growl, then look at their master. But if the groundsman didn't twig or say anything, someone else did.

Anne was delivering fish; a customer kindly asked "Would you like some apples dear?" Anne innocently replied "No thank you we have plenty, my brothers get them." She was speaking to the groundsman's sister!

Police Constable Steer was well known to us and we were well known to him. He was a good man, at the end of his long career. One Saturday morning Ted, Terry, Bob and I were on our way home carrying the weekly shopping. Bob was pushing his beloved bicycle, all four of us were having a Woodbine, the still air was full of smoke from our efforts to blow smoke rings. Around the corner he came peddling hard up the hill. With the exception of Bob's our weekly fags went over the hedge, Bob pushing his into the handlebars of his bike, still alight. PC got off his highly polished steed, it didn't need Sherlock Holmes to smell the tobacco-filled air and see guilt all over our faces.

"You boys been smoking?"

We were law-abiding Sunday School lads, honest as the day is long. "No Mr Steer, not us," hoping the hedge didn't catch fire. "We don't smoke, my Dad would give us a hiding if we did." I looked down, smoke was pouring out of the handlebars of Bob's bike. I quickly put my hand over one end, Bob did the same with the other.

We had bluffed our way out of that one, or so we thought and went on around the corner. PC Steer headed off up the hill.

Three of us were 'fag less', Bob was going to retrieve his at all cost. He stood the bike on the back wheel, banged it up and down, left and right, and dropped it on to the road, until out it popped, still alight, just. He bent down to pick it up but was beaten at the post; by the time it took him to let go of the handlebars, drop the bike on to the road and bend down, PC Steer had grabbed it first. His bike was well oiled, we hadn't seen or heard him, so intrigued we were with Bob's antics.

Nothing was said, that man had a nose for being in the right place at the right time. If we had a salmon peel in the net, he would just happen to be there, sitting on the shore, waiting. That's the way things were back then, with policemen and Sunday School lads.

This time our friendly bobby seemed, just a little more officious in his manner: "Are your parents in?" Sixth sense told us that apple pinching was on his agenda.

"Mr Steer how nice to see you." Mum said, in her voice used for special occasions, and special people. "Please come in."

"I have reason to believe that your boys have been helping themselves to apples from Mr Holman's orchard." (This is a true account of the next half hour's events, every word written was spoken, every action took place).

"There's a nasty cough you have Constable," then as quick as lightning, Mum took down a bottle of mead, made by Dad from honey fortified with gin and other concoctions. At the same time she turned to us, grabbed a bag and whispered "Quick, go and get some apples while I keep him talking."

Later we pushed our local Bobby's bicycle up the drive for him, and after failing to mount his steed twice, we watched as he walked unsteadily up the road. Rumour had it that he slept in a barn at Harcourt Farm until tea time.

The evening meal was a gathering of the family; the day's happenings were discussed, latest war news mulled over and so on. Not one of us asked to be excused from the table as the meal ended. Dad was finishing his second helping of apple tart and custard, and a breathless hush filled the room.

"We had a visitor today, dear" said Mum, "Police Constable Steer. The boys have been taking one or two apples from the orchard."

'One or two!' We had been having apple this and apple that for weeks, and yet I should mention in our defence, that we only took windfalls. There had been quite a few windy days of late, and the ground was still covered.

These are not, nor could they be the exact words Dad used, but the gist is the same. "Did you ask if we could take some?" He asked.

Anne answered, "Yes I asked when delivering fish and he didn't answer, just thanked me for the fish and walked away."

Dad – full up with apple tart and looking to see if there was any chance of a second helping was in his element. He chose every word, every sentence, he was the prosecutor and defender at the same time, he knew, and was right, that his response would be remembered well into the future.

"If we take anything that belongs to another person without their consent that is theft, in this case the law has been broken. In peace time I would never condone such action, however we are not living in peace time. We need no reminder that it is important to uphold the law, but in these difficult times a little bending of the rules is required. For instance, we often go out after dark to check the net, yet two nights a week, while on duty with the River Patrol it is our duty to stop this very thing happening." He looked at me, losing his thread a little, he added in his schoolmaster's voice; "The penalties are severe!"

Concluding he said, "In my book deliberate waste of food, should be frowned upon, I will have a word with Police Constable Steer."

Living in Cornwall was one long holiday. The countryside with its lanes, fields, wooded areas not to mention the estuary, its shoreline and boating, we neither required or asked for anything more. However when a day out in the car to Land's End was suggested it was hard to contain our excitement.

It was to be Anne's and Jean's combined birthday treat, a picnic at the very end of England, about forty-five miles away, a two-hour drive. There was to be no speeding, Mum's orders, no Kodak on government orders. Memories we have, photographs we have not.

The great day arrived at last, the old jalopy was loaded and given a pre-trip inspection, engine oil dipstick lifted out, twice, tyres checked, oil can squirted on anything and everything that moved, sparkplugs given the once over, engine started advance and retard levers tinkered with, we were clear for takeoff.

It wasn't then just a case of get in, switch on the engine and off. This was probably only the fifth or sixth time we had been out in her. This was a special treat. Although we would see towns and a city, villages and farms, it was the car that took centre stage. There were children in those days who had never ridden in a motor car, we were the privileged ones. Just think never having heard the whining of a gearbox, or axle, smelt the oil and leather.

Miss Sampson ran a general store at the road junction where the road to Feock joins the main road from Truro.

"Let's see if she has any sweets," suggested Mum.

We stopped. Although sweets were on coupons, producing your ration book in no way guaranteed your quota. If there were any sweets to be had then you were lucky, if not then it was just one of those things. It wasn't uncommon that for six months sweets were unobtainable, and when they were available it was a case of queuing perhaps for an hour or more.

Miss Sampson's shop was a fascination, we loved it. Tucked away behind her house, if it were not for the odd enamel sign outside on the wall passersby could easily miss it. It was her pride and joy, her life. It possessed one thing that today is so hard to find, the smell of foods: from bread to onions, cheese to bacon, and it was all there. No plastic or refrigerators; tills were wooden drawers, all immaculately kept. If items were out of stock – and they very often were – advertising posters or empty boxes took their place on the shelves. Often an empty Fry's chocolate box was placed where the real thing should have been, just to remind us of days past, and dream of days to come.

On the counter in this 'real' shop was a pair of scales, highly polished, which were for us the centre of attraction. Standing in a line, our noses at counter height, we held our breath as this dear shopkeeper weighed the exact amount, and I mean exact, with a scoopful of the customer's requirements. She would shake it into an open paper bag. Little by little, slowly the needle would record too little, or too much. Not a smile, no expression, not a word was uttered; concentration was paramount, fairness had to be achieved, every customer had their entitlement, and that is what they had, no more, no less, than the exact amount. As the needle moved towards top dead centre we all held our breath.

One Saturday morning, as per routine, Ted, Terry Bob and I were collecting the weekly shopping. Lentils were being weighed, in and out of the bag they were added or taken away. Ted broke the long silence: "Why don't you cut one in half?" Miss Sampson didn't flinch, her expression didn't change, then as the needle steadied, with a Mona Liza-type smile she took one lentil held, it between her finger and thumb, and dropped it in to the bag. We loved her so; she knew every Saturday that the Woodbines we bought were for us.

So on again to Land's End. It was our lucky day; we had sweets, one each on the way there and another on the way home. Through villages and towns people returned our waves, through road blocks manned by military personnel who were always ready with a cheeky remark. Passing through Penzance and on out into the rugged moors where trees are shaped by, and lean away from the strong prevailing winds. Passing granite built houses and stone built walls framing small fields, until finally, we could see the Atlantic Ocean.

Land's End from the air, as it would have looked when the author visited in 1941.

The sliding roof of the car was pulled back, and standing on a stool we took it in turns standing up with our heads out in the bracing sea air, which had a much saltier tang to it then, or so I believe.

All around us were the old tin mines. Dad said that men had laboured far out under the ocean, they could hear the sea roaring above, and salt water seeped into the mine. This, he said, was the birthplace of the Cornish pasty.

We stopped at Sennen for petrol – the garage is still there today. I remember Dad telling the attendant that during the Great War petrol was two shillings and eleven pence a gallon, and motorists would insist that the last drip of fuel went into the tank, they both agreed that those day's would never return.

On again just one mile to go, we had a picnic, a birthday tea, on the edge of the cliff, overlooking the waves below. Beyond the Longships Lighthouse three coasters were rounding the head-

land before making their way up the English Channel, the largest of them had a tall funnel aft which was belching black smoke, Mary stood watching them for a while, her dress and hair blowing in the wind, and then she recited the last verse of John Masefield's 'Cargoes'.

Dirty British coaster with a salt-caked smoke stack,
Butting up the Channel in the mad March days,
With a cargo of Tyne coal, road-rails, pig lead,
Firewood, iron-ware, and cheap tin trays.

Due to her experiences during the blitz Mary's' childhood memories became spasmodic, she was soon to forget that fine poem, and the day she used the cliffs at Land's End as her stage. I can think of nothing more tragic.

A seagull hovered overhead on the upcurrent of air, moving its tail very slightly one way and then the other; it rose slightly on the updraft, and then

49

The petrol station at Sennen.

dropped again, flirting with the wind, for no other reason than the sheer enjoyment of doing so.

On the way home that day, we were approaching Sennen, and just before we reached the petrol station, a lady stepped out into the road, and held out her hand. Stopping and getting out, in those days it was not considered the 'done thing' to speak to a lady through a car window, she handed Dad our petrol cap. "My Husband asked me to give you this," she said "you were so busy chatting that you forgot it." Thanking her Dad asked how she knew that we would return, "You were the only car that went down there, and you couldn't get back any other way!"

The trip to Land's End was our last outing in the old jalopy. Mum broke the news at tea, "The car has gone, two men called, they said it was being requisitioned, and converted into an ambulance, they paid me fifteen pounds compensation for it."

Nothing was said, Dad made no comment or showed signs of his loss. The Wolseley was more to us than just a means of transport, rarely used for the purpose it was built for, due to cost, eighteen miles per gallon downhill with a following wind.

She had been part of the family, used as a plaything on wet days, taken out of the garage and run over with an oily rag on warm sunny days. Just like the *Swordfish* she had a soul, and I can prove it – when reaching thirty miles per hour, she shook with excitement!

Perhaps I shouldn't reveal our private thoughts – the four kids' suspicions were that fifteen pounds might have changed hands, plus a large piece of white paper on which was beautifully inscribed in the very best copperplate 'Five Pounds' had ended up in someone's apron pocket – the granddaughter of a Somerset horse dealer perhaps!

Dad bought a Norton 'saddletank' motor bike, a sports job, and we spent hours helping to restore it. Mr Polglaze built new parts on his lathe, everything on it was stripped down. Another similar model was found, clutch plates rebuilt using corks from bottles, and so two old bikes became one.

Finally the shining repainted machine was ready for a test flight, neighbours gathered, pilot dressed in leather flying hat and goggles, sporting a Flying Officer Kite's moustache, sat proudly astride, twiddling levers on the handlebars. Standing astride, foot on the kick-start lever, all his weight thrown down his right leg – nothing, again nothing. Carburettor needle given a tweak, kick, bang! Backfire, smoke everywhere except out of the exhaust pipe. Dad was lifted off the ground, I cannot say how high he flew, two three feet perhaps, it wasn't the going up that mattered, it was the coming down, the saddle was made of thick leather and held up by two heavily built springs!

Children had a lot of respect for their parents and their feelings in those days, but I couldn't help it, and anyway the others shouldn't have laughed, "I bet that hurt him more than it hurt me," that's all I said.

Not to put too fine a point on it, I wasn't keen on the motor bike, often I was given a lift on the back of it to school, Dad rigged out in leather hat goggles, long trousers, me on the back wearing, sports coat, shorts, and school cap. I would tuck in behind him as close as possible for protection from the slipstream, this ex Bristol fighter pilot, pretending to be flying a Spitfire, would go like a bat out of hell. Two large farm dogs would be lying in wait, they could hear the roar of the exhaust a long way off, and had time to plan their strategy, and plan of attack. Coming at us from both sides of the road, they would start to race ahead of their quarry, until one was one side and the other the other side at the same time, teeth inches away from bare legs. Dad devised a plan. Wait until the exact moment, adjust the advance lever, throttle right back. Then when dog's nose and exhaust outlet were in line, throttle wide open. BANG! Have you ever seen a dog try to stop dead at thirty-five mph?

I only caught a sight of one, somersaulting end over end. That was the last we ever saw of them.

If the dogs were not enough to contend with, racing was. A work colleague of Dad's had a water-cooled Scott motorbike, and there was a friendly rivalry between them as to which was the fastest of the two bikes. Remember there was little traffic on the roads then, we had the track to ourselves, often meeting at Playing Place down the hill towards Truro we would race, under the railway bridge, right hand turning, climb - stick back a little right rudder, foot rest inches away from the road, eyes closed, 'G' forces felt in the belly regions. I can tell you by the time we touched down on Lemon Quay, I had reached the 'Amen' bit.

We had a distant relation and her two children staying for a short while and to simplify meals and so on, a pool system regarding food and rationing was established. One can only imagine the size of beef that Dad tied on to the carrier of his motor-bike that Saturday, eleven rations-worth!

The problem was that when he arrived home, that very large joint of beef was gone, disappeared, not there, no newspaper wrapping or string. No matter how many times he looked it did not reappear, and Mum was walking up the drive to meet him.

We were painting the boat near the garage, "John," he shouted "quick jump on the back, you look left, I'll look right." I was keen to help find that chunk of fat-covered beef for no other reason than the dripping it would produce, a stone jar full, spread on toast, sprinkled with a liberal helping of salt, cut off a block with a bread knife, brown dripping. It makes my mouth water just thinking about it. Slowly for once, we set off back to Truro. But there was an urgency – the boat had been pulled out of the water for a paint job, and tomorrow was Sunday. No fish, no beef, in fact no Sunday lunch. On we went past the area where the dogs had carried out their attacks, on down the hill towards Truro, nothing, not a sausage! Dad had two options, the Foreign Legion or the Police Station, and he chose the latter. Rationing there was, shortages there were, but one thing was not in short supply during those war years – honesty. Police Stations' lost and found departments were always busy then. If the joint had been found the chances of it being there were high, it had been found, and it was there.

However! Let's look at it from the Police Sergeant on duty's point of view. A large joint of beef had been handed in. It was only natural that the 'Black Market' was suspected, then in walked Biggles looking as if he had lost sixpence and found a tanner, and to cap it all was accompanied by a boy with green paint over his hands and clothes, and with oil splashed all over his legs from a motor bike driving chain.

We were taken into separate rooms. They loosened my tongue with a hot drink and light-hearted laughter. How many brothers and sisters did I have? Did I know PC Steer? I emptied my pockets, one silver cigarette lighter, one penknife, a piece of string, a 303 shell cartridge, loose airgun pellets. These are the items I remember, others I have forgotten. We were released, no 'going up before the beak'.

We were on our way home, Sunday's joint tucked down between us. Those living at that time in Playing Place, or near the Punch Bowl and Ladle Pub, plus properties in between, were given a treat, a motor bike that sounded like a thousand air raid sirens, ridden by a character singing 'Tom Bowling' at the top of his voice.

Once again Christmas left us with a special memory. 1941 had been a traumatic year where memories are concerned. We had experienced war at the sharp end, emerging as 'free range children'.

The United States of America had entered the war, a special period of history was about to enter our lives. Christmas is always a time to reflect, and look forward to the future, never more so than it was then

Making puddings was a ritual. Rations were saved months beforehand, we knew that pudding-making time signalled the start of the 'run up' to Christmas. Each of us was granted one wish as we took the wooden spoon and had a stir, and if mum wasn't looking a quick dip of the finger and a taste.

It was a tradition that a silver threepenny coin was added to the pudding mix, and it was considered lucky if it ended up on your plate. However at Christmas 1941 a change was made, silver charms replaced the silver coin. I only remember one charm, a bachelor button. Each of us searched the Christmas pudding on our plate, one by one the silver charms were found, all except the bachelor button which, tradition has it, forecast that the finder would never marry. June had already made her views clear by saying that she would rather not have any pudding than find the button; however she relented at the last moment when Dad pointed out that the odds of her finding it were eight to one.

Plates were cleared, all except one, June's. All eyes were on her as she slowly cleared her plate, nothing, last spoonful, still nothing, a cry went up "She's swallowed it".

Every Christmas for years later that day was recalled "Remember when June swallowed the bachelor button!" Even after she had married for

the third time she was still reminded, and always denied, that she had 'swallowed the button'. Until, fifty years later, I finally got a confession, no, not from June, from Mum who owned up. The button was produced from her purse, she had kept it all those years and our suspicions were founded: the button had never gone into the china bowl filled with pudding mixture.

During the winter months we – the four – went to bed early, not to sleep but to read, either to ourselves or to one another. Bob had read 'Billy the Barrage Balloon' so many times he knew it off by heart, page after page word perfect. Anne could recite verses from Longfellow's 'The Song of Hiawatha'. We were competitive with one another and helpful at the same time. We had no audience, just ourselves, although I think our parents often listened from the bottom of the stairs.

Then we had a brainwave, why not hold a concert in aid of the Mission to Seamen; we were already involved in local fund raising activities, collecting for a jumble sale in the village hall and so on. Mrs Hadley, who lived in a bungalow on the Devoran side of the Point, was the area fund raising representative for the Mission to Seamen, a worthy cause near to our hearts. All monies collected would be handed to her. We had the venue, our garage, the car was gone after all, and the motor bike could be wheeled outside. The more we talked the more enthusiastic we became.

At the back of the garage was a large wooden frame on top of which stood a water storage tank. If we covered it with sacking it would be ideal for a 'waiting to perform' venue.

This was to be a live show in every sense of the word, no program, no rehearsals, or order of appearance, and no compere. It was a case of all squeezing in the area under the water tank and pushing the next performer out, saying "You next".

Advertising was by word of mouth, apart from a few hand-painted posters pinned up in the local area. We had full support from neighbours, each doing their bit; chairs and benches were lent, a sign painted, 'entrance one shilling'.

A larger and more professional show was being staged in Feock, 'If You Go Down in the Woods Today' in which most of us had a part to play, and so we were anxious to get our production over. One Saturday the idea came to us, the next we were on stage. It must be a world record, and probably the first live show ever held at Restronguet Point, and, I suspect the last. The garage is still there, exactly as it was then.

Saturday arrived, with more customers than we had bargained for; the doors would have to be left open to accommodate the overflow. The ferry from The Pandora was loaded down to the gunnels, had we bitten off more than we could chew?

What a mixture of folk filled that garage: Mr Ferris, dressed in his fishing gear, stood with a Major in full dress uniform, standing at the back with a member of the Home Guard who carried a rifle. A farmer proudly stood with his injured son who was dressed in a blue suit and a red tie, the 'uniform' of an injured serviceman.

Ted started first, wearing a pair of bell bottom trousers and *the* sailors hat. He sang 'I'm Popeye the Sailor Man', followed by Anne dressed as a squaw, reciting from her beloved, 'The Song of Hiawatha'.

> *On the shores of Gitche Gumee*
> *Of the shining Big-Sea-Water*
> *Stood Nokomis, the old woman,*

> *Pointing with her finger Westward*
> *O'-er the water pointing westward*
> *To the purple clouds of sunset.*

– and so on.

Anne was a hard act to follow, however Bob and Jean sang a duet of a popular song, everyone sang it from marching soldiers to delivery boys; it was the 1940s 'Top of the Pops':

> *In the store, in the store*
> *There was jam, jam mixed up with the ham,*
> *In the Quartermasters Store,*
> *My eyes are dim I cannot see,*
> *I have not brought my specs with me...*

The audience joined in, making up their versions, 'there were eggs, eggs walking about on legs' etc. The performance was a success – I believe it was not only for the entertainment value, but for those present who had concerns over the effects the war might be having on the younger generation; those doubts were put to rest, the answer was given, children everywhere had taken everything thrown at them in their stride.

I dressed as a scarecrow, and recited a Walter De La Mare poem, as taught by a part time lady teacher at school who at one time was an actress.

Two photographs, not of our concert but one that we took part in at Feock at that time. On the opposite page from left to right: looking at the picture, third (with a pointed hat) is Jean, the smart looking chap with a straw hat is Bob, forth from the right kneeling, is Anne, the tall girl on the right is Mary. Above: another picture of the play in which Bob played the groom, and his bride was Joy Cox, an evacuee, who lived with Mrs James.

As I recited the last verse I walked through the audience, through the door, taking large strides: "I watched him striding, lank behind his clashing team, and know soon will the wheat swish body high, where once lay sterile snow."

I would like to record that I had a standing ovation, but I didn't: the reason being that more than half the audience had nowhere to sit!

The poems we recited are still remembered today. The show ended with a lot of clapping, and speeches. We were taken to Falmouth where at the Mission to Seamen hostel we were introduced to Merchant Navy Seamen whose ship had been torpedoed. After tea we all sang that raising hymn, 'For Those In Peril on the Sea'.

Before this war would was over, there would be other occasions where that hymn would be sung, not only in church and school, we also enjoyed singing it when rowing our boat, we knew the words off by heart.

We were presented with a Mission to Seamen Blue Ribbon medal, although we were proud and honoured to have received it, we had done nothing more than have a laugh.

Chapter 6

EYE WITNESS

Not wishing to doubt others who record history, especially the great man himself, I have deliberated long and hard as to whether I should add my twopenny's worth to a World War II mystery: Which route did Winston Churchill fly on the final leg of his historic flight across the Atlantic Ocean in a Boeing Berwick flying boat in January 1942.

Churchill himself believed a navigational error had taken them to within 'five or six minutes' flying time of German gun batteries at Brest. Historians doubt this, saying that the aircraft probably flew just south of the Lizard. There was no navigational error by Kelly Rogers the pilot, or by any member of his crew, the aircraft was nowhere near Brest, or the Lizard.

I cannot say where the flying boat first crossed the Cornish coast that day, however, what I can say is, it was nowhere near the Lizard. It passed to the south of Truro flew down over the Roseland Peninsula over the channel coast near Porthcurno passing south of Dodman Point, then I presume-

A sketch of the flying boat, escorted by fighters, passing over Cornwall with Winston Churchill aboard on his flight home from Bermuda.

up the Channel until turning north into Plymouth sound.

Boeing 'Berwick' flying boat similar to that which carried Winston Churchill across the Atlantic.

How can I be so certain? I saw it, and so did my brother, sisters, mother, and two of my friends, plus two school friends who lived at Porthscatho, and who had watched as it passed over the coast, heading out over the sea towards Plymouth.

We heard them first, yes them, a large flying boat escorted by four or five Spitfires. They were not flying in formation, the fighters were flying in circles, ahead then behind, above then below, rolling over and over they portrayed excitement, sheer joy, like dolphins playing around a small craft. We shared those four Spitfire pilots' excitement Mum shouted "That must be 'Winny', he's back." The BBC confirmed it the next day.

We watched that historic flight until it disappeared over the hill behind St Just in Roseland. At first we wrongly identified the flying boat as a Sunderland, but from the outset it looked larger, and we had never seen a Berwick before. However, for those who lived in the area at that time, there is absolutely no doubt Winston Churchill flew over Cornwall that day.

As children, we filled Rudyard Kipling's 'unforgiving minute'. If we couldn't find adventure, then, adventure found us. It was a dull January Saturday morning, the boat was still out of the water for the winter, not a lot on, no plans, but there was always the shore with its beachcombing 'finds', or trees to climb.

We could hear it; soon we would smell it, a boy's magnet, and music to our ears: a Fordson Standard tractor, heading our way, down the hill at its top speed of three mph.

We loved that tractor and its stocky driver, with his sailor's cap covered in oil. He had slowness about his nature, nothing was ever done in a hurry. Jack had spent some time in Canada, and in conversation always ended a sentence by adding "partner". "That's right partner," or "Thank you partner," and so on. He was the first person we had ever met who had visited far off lands, and loved to hear him reminisce.

"I once went into a saloon and entered a raffle for a horse, and I won it. However when I called to pick it up it was dead and buried, and I paid for the burial! Guess what partner, everybody who had bought a ticket had become the legal owner and had to stump up burial costs! One moonlit night we armed ourselves with shovels, and guess what partners, there was no horse, just a heap of soil."

We were in hysterics. "What did you do Jack?"

"Took the first boat home to England, partner. Canadians didn't take to kindly to having one of theirs roughed up."

Every ten minutes, Jack would wipe his hands on a piece of rag, undo his army gas mask case, take out a tin Thermos flask, pour about one tablespoonful of tea into a cup, take about ten little sips, then go through all the rigmarole of packing away the contents of his lunch bag, threading the webbing straps, and so on.

Then the work started unloading the small trailer. Paraffin and petrol cans, tarpaulins, tools, jacks, ropes and so on, until at last the plough. A lot of heaving, getting out of the way, getting in the way, then the long bit, taking off the oak road protectors (the tractor was fitted with spade lugs and to prevent the road being damaged large wooden wheels were bolted around the circumference, and to remove these the rear of the tractor had to be jacked up).

The land we ploughed then is worth about two hundred pounds per square foot today. Beautiful houses now stand where once oats swayed in the wind; the view demands a high premium.

We were privileged living there, having that view. And standing on the platform of a tractor that sounded like a thousand tin cans being towed behind the Flying Scotsman passing through a tunnel, we had it all.

Seagulls played dare, trying to grab a worm from the turning furrow, their beaks bright yellow and orange, and feathers that shone in the sun. They were not the same as today's scavengers of council tips, their natural food was in abundance then: fish from unpolluted seas, worms from soil treated only with basic slag, a by-product of the steel industry.

As Jack drove the tractor we pulled the rope that lowered and raised the plough. Perhaps there was an element of danger standing in front of a plough, but danger then was second nature to us, the only way to be one hundred per cent safe was to stay in bed with the blanket pulled up over your head.

Over the next year or so we grew strong enough to drive the tractor, starting first with harrowing and rolling we progressed to the more difficult task of ploughing. Jack would start with the first round or two, then we would take over. Ploughing a straight furrow was an art and however hard we tried, our master would say "looks like a dog peeing in the snow, partner."

Soon the corn would grow body high; it would be harvest time, our favourite.

Barrage Balloons that protected Falmouth and all major towns and cities from low-level aerial attacks, were occasionally struck by lightning. We watched as they slowly fell to earth, nearly always burning out before hitting the ground.

We didn't see it, neither did we know where it came from, the wind was light, blowing from an easterly direction, certainly not strong enough to cause a balloon to 'break free'. It must have silently drifted across the estuary, and in all probability would have continued on its last journey unnoticed by ourselves, had three Spitfires not appeared on the scene.

We lay back on the grass, and watched in awe at the scene unfolding in the sky above us. Practice perhaps, deliberately removing a hazard maybe, reasons we would never know, but one thing is for sure, they were enjoying every second. Diving from above one at a time they gave the poor balloon a burst of cannon fire. I say 'poor' because it looked like a dying whale, helpless at the mercy of the finest and most loved aircraft of its day, flown by the cream of young men, five thousand feet above us.

How did we know they were flying at that height? Simple, we used the same mathematical principle Dad had taught us when establishing how far away lightning was. Sound travels about one mile in five seconds, and so as the cannon of the Spitfires flashed we counted. Counting to five meant the sound had reached us from a mile above or approximately five thousand feet.

Slowly the balloon deflated and started to descend, losing its shape. Its fins drooped, there was an air of sadness as we watched it die. The pilots rolled and looped the loop, victory was theirs. The Battle of Britain had been won some time before, and for them there would be battles ahead, but the task in hand that day was 'a piece of cake'.

It might have been weeks or even months before it dawned on us, we just didn't think of it

at the time, those Spitfires were diving and firing at the balloon right above our heads, we were in the line of fire, just lying there on the grass one mile below.

Police Constable Steer's wartime log records the following, "I was near the Punch Bowl and Ladle Inn when a Barrage Balloon fell out of the sky."

Over the winter and early spring of 1942 there were several modifications made to the *Swordfish*, the most important of which was a new sail, a balanced lug, stepped forward. Made by a friend at Restronguet Weir, the theory was that we would be able to sail into the wind more efficiently, and it proved to be quite successful. Mr Hartnell built a removable platform from driftwood which was placed over the stern. This had many uses, we placed the net on it which enabled it to be set by one person. Just drop the weight over the side, row, and over went the net, no problem!

The new platform became the bridge; the helmsman stood on it and steered with an oar, and by moving his stance he was able to use his weight to help stabilize the boat. 'Heath Robinson' it might have looked, but efficient it was.

I don't remember the date, or for that matter the time of the year, but we – my friends and I – never forgot the events of the next few days. How could we?

The older ones of us, Ted Blackburn, John Salmon and yours truly were putting the *Swordfish,* with her new sail, through her paces. The wind was fresh, from the west, and we hugged the shore sailing towards Looe Beach then turning headed for Mylor Harbour, and back again. Each time we lost ground going further out into the estuary, until we were off the mouth of Pill Creek. Right lets go! Sail pulled in tight, the tide flowing with us which would stop her drifting off course as we passed the mouths of Restronguet and Mylor Creeks. The wind was fresher here away from the lee of the land.

Our average age was twelve years, we knew it all, there was no worry of having the young ones on board for us to take care of, we were strong swimmers, and we were showing off. There would be one retired sea captain who lived at Mylor Weir looking through his 'glass' – as he called it – he would be watching our every action.

A damp mist was in the air, together with the spray of the sea as we cut through the water dampening our hair and clothes.

John S had the sheet (rope) that held the sail, wrapped around the stern seat. If things got too hairy he could let it go. I leaned on the oar, balancing her every move. Her gunnels were level with the sea, she had the bit between her teeth, and I was shaking through a mixture of excitement and anticipation. The *Swordfish* was in charge like a runaway horse, nothing could stop us, or would it?

We were heading towards Pennarow Point when we saw it, a seaplane, not more than five hundred yards dead ahead, it was very close in to the shore, dark in colour, and its engines were running.

Aircraft recognition was second nature to us, all schoolboys, and many girls, could identify an aircraft type at a glance. One passing through a break in the clouds was enough, friend or foe, fighter or bomber, it made little difference. Sometimes just the sound of its engines was enough, our lives could depend on it. But this seaplane, dark in colour with two engines, had no markings.

We were baffled, action and quick thinking was required, the *Swordfish* would not sail into the nearest shore, Mylor, because that was up-wind. Turning and getting out of there, going back the way we had come, was probably the best option, however, to do so faced the risk of stalling while turning, plus we would be side-on to the strange looking aircraft. There was only one option left, running downwind and making for a freighter

This is an official aircraft recognition model of a Heinkel He115, and is more than likely the aircraft we saw, however it was never positively identified.

that had been badly damaged and was aground off the St Mawes coast. We let out the sail, pointed her bow at the freighter and 'ran with it', keeping an eye on the mystery plane.

"A Catalina," suggested Ted.

"The floats are different," said John Salmon, the most knowledgeable aircraft buff. "Italian I'd say."

It aircraft had a long canopy with a machine gun mounted; its motors were revving up. It turned, travelled out into the mouth of the estuary about three hundred yards or so, stopped for a little while then went back into the shore. Three or four minutes later it repeated the whole operation, moving out stopping then returning. Three times it did this then it finally turned, pointed out to sea and opened up its motors. Taxiing out into the open water she took off, flying at only twenty feet or so above the sea and finally disappearing from view. The sea plane was never positively identified, however, over the following days, pawing over our aircraft recognition books we believe it was a Heinkel He115.

Was this the mystery plane seen that day on the river? A Heinkel He115 takes off.

We were in a dilemma should we head for the shore and run to St Mawes find someone, anyone, who could telephone the authorities in Falmouth, whoever they were. Although we hadn't seen any markings we were certain the seaplane was up to no good, that someone should be informed, but who? This was a time when 'Careless talk cost lives'.

We had never been to St Mawes, the chances of seeing a policeman or a naval officer were, as far as we knew, slim. Added to which we had no shoes on. Picture it, three bare-footed boys, unknown to the locals, running around like headless chickens looking for, well, anyone who looked 'official', to tell them that the Germans had landed across the water at Mylor. I think not!

So we decided to row home as fast as we could, to where we were known. I must point out here that not one of us had ever used a telephone, and didn't have any money. There were no 999 facilities then, and as far as we were aware not one house had a telephone installed. There were no chains of command, no, 'if you see anything suspicious call this number or that number'. No, wind a handle tell the old biddy at the other end, that you are twelve years old, and that three of us had seen a German plane that could be laying mines in a shipping lane.

Most neighbours were polite and listened, one laughed. But we knew someone who would at least listen, Mr Ferris.

A finer man would be hard to find; oyster trawler man in the winter time, mackerel fisherman in the summer, we had often spoken to him, and he to us, as equals. We helped him bring his day's catch up the beach, often scrubbed oil off his white boat, and begged him to take us with him to the Manacles rocks fishing. The answer was always the same as given by the skipper of the *Shamrock*, "leave those waters to us old uns."

I have often wondered at what sights Mr Ferris, and other fishermen would have seen, from the mackerel fishing grounds off the Manacles rocks. There they would be only a short distance from Lizard Point; large convoys would pass close by. U-boats operated in these waters, low-flying aircraft patrolled these important shipping lanes, and yet not once did he ever relate to us stories we would have loved to hear.

A painting by John Edgar Platt, RSMA – now in the Imperial War Museum – is of a convoy passing the Lizard, where just a mile away Mr Ferris fished for mackerel.

We were about to find out the reason first hand, why we were always told, "beyond your imposed boundary, is best left to the old uns."

We told Mr Ferris all that we had seen that day, locations, time; we answered his many questions.

"They had chosen a location out of sight from Falmouth, Mylor, or St Mawes," he said, almost to himself, nodding his head, he said. "Clever, leave it with me." And so we did.

Two or perhaps three days later we were cleaning the net and Mum was hanging out the washing, just a normal day. Cutting inside the Black Rock was a coaster, heading up-Channel. She was in a hurry taking the shortest route. Guessing, I'd say that she was about 500 tons, a work horse of the coastal trade, carrying anything from coal, to timber, scrap metal to corn; you name it they carried it.

Her engines were noisy, a deep throated "pop pop" sound, a single cylinder job by the sound of it. The weather was calm, the thumping of the exhaust carrying across the water. Such vessels were common and we continued with the job in hand. The sound of the explosion and shock waves took about five seconds to reach us, and by the time we looked up to where she had been there was nothing but a narrow column of spray, no fire, or smoke, just water. I'm guessing now – 150 feet plus of sea water rose into the sky where seconds before a little ship and her crew had been. The column pointed to the sky, hovered there for a split second before falling back from whence it came. Mum had run down the garden and stood above us, at the edge of the cliff, pointing, and crying, "It disappeared, I saw it, those poor men."

I briefly looked up then back again towards an almost empty sea; there were one or two black dots in the water, nothing more – at the very spot, where, just a day or two previously we had seen the seaplane.

When we next met Mr Ferris his face said it all, - "Don't ask, please don't ask," was all he said. He just walked up the shore, and went home; he knew we would see to his gear.

The next day we helped Mr Ferris clean oil from his boat – he told us that he was the first on the scene, and had pulled one of the injured survivors

The ship's binnacle, which together with its badly damaged wooden stand washed ashore at Looe Beach.
Courtesy Mr and Mrs C Gilbert, Feock.

from the oily water, three of whose comrades had lost their lives, and two others had horrendous wounds. A binnacle, its stand splintered, washed ashore on Looe Beach and later an unidentified body washed ashore. Local people collected and he was given a Christian burial at St Feock Church.

That's the way things were during the war; bodies were the responsibility of local councils. There were no post-mortems or inquests, in all probability the families of the men who lost their lives that day were unaware that their loved one rests in one of the most beautiful churchyards in Cornwall.

Mr Ferris and his little white boat had passed over the mine at least four times; although of course it could have been a magnetic type, detonated by a metal hull.

Life continued, throughout 1942, war and growing up progressing side by side, often fishing, often aircraft spotting. There were times when we would be out in the boat and a German reconnaissance aircraft would fly over head, high up. Anti- aircraft guns would open up, we could see the shell bursts either ahead, behind or very near, although the guns were over a mile away, we would shout instructions, "aim ahead, left, no, ahead," and so on. Unlike Plymouth were never saw a hit, many near misses but no smoke or parachutes, they should have given us a gun or two. Which reminds me of 'the day of the gun'.

Oystercatchers fishing off the coast. It was in a boat like these that Mr Ferris rescued the injured seaman from the water just to the right of Black Rock (just visible in the far distance).

The author's sketch of a German plane surrounded by puffs of bursting anti-aircraft shells.

Before the outbreak of hostilities, Uncle Jack gave Dad a large, very large, muzzle-loading shotgun. One day, ignoring Mum's sound advice, "be careful what you are doing with that gun Jimmy," it was taken out of the coal house and down to the water's edge.

"That damn cormorant has had more than his fair share of my fish," Dad said, and we watched as the gun was loaded; first the correct measure of gunpowder was poured into the barrel, then a cotton wad. Both were rammed down hard, then the round shot, another wad, and once again the ram rod did its bit. Finally a brass firing cap was put in place, the cormorant watched with interest.

Bang! Smoke and what must have been coal dust, filled the air. Something frightened the bird which took off, flew about fifty feet, landed, dived under the water, then surfaced again, just feet away.

As far as we could see it was in better shape than Dad! How can anyone be pale and black at the same time? He was.

The gun was put back into the coal house, and we all had the common sense not to broach the subject of muzzle-loading cannons again. However the story doesn't end there.

We took the gun Anne, Jean – in fact all the gang – every one of us was guilty. We had some knowledge of guns and we reasoned that Dad had not put enough gunpowder in. The shot must have just fallen out of the end of the barrel. "Just leave it to the experts," we thought.

The net was set; the cormorant was having a late breakfast. Twice the measure of ingredients was rammed down the barrel, and a little more for good luck, the big muzzle-loading shot gun was lashed to 'our' tree, and a long piece of string was wrapped around the trigger. We were about to kill, pluck, and gut that fish-thief in one go, or so we thought.

Now a couple of us – or three at the most – had often said that we could have brought down a German aircraft given an anti-aircraft gun, but it took six of us to carry out a plan that would fill the air with feathers and other stuff from a defenceless bird, one to take aim, two who would give the command to fire at the exact moment, one to pull the string, and the sixth would keep an eye open for Mum.

Silence, pure, silence, as we waited for the 'go ahead',

The command was given: Now, pull! ...nothing, no bang, and no feathers. A second try nothing, and a third, new caps were placed where caps on guns are placed, still nothing. Desperation now, bird or no bird, we had to get rid of the contents of the blunderbuss.

Suggestions were made as to how we could remove the gunpowder and shot; after all if Dad ever tried to frighten a bird again, or a German airman was spotted, he would ram a third quota of gunpowder down the barrel, and it wouldn't be a motorbike backfiring in this quiet corner of England. No sir, we were in big trouble.

"Drop a lighted roll of paper down the barrel," said one. "Light a fire and place the gun on it," suggested another, and so on. Until Bob, the youngest of us, came up with a sure-fire solution, "Put it back in the coal house and say nothing." And so that was decided upon.

Over the years that followed our parents moved three or four times, always the family heirloom, complete with its contents went with them, until it finally found what could have been its last resting place, over a large open fireplace in the lounge of the Star Castle Hotel, St Mary's on the Isles Of Scilly.

When I confessed to Mr Stevenson the hotel owner, it was taken out to sea and ceremonially dropped over the side near a large rock where cormorants dry their wings.

Our fishing net was set at right angles to the shore; both ends were held in place with either a small anchor or a large stone. The total length was somewhere in the region of fifty feet. The total catch varied widely, anything from six fish, up to one hundred, depending on the time of year. Autumn was the best time, the sea had warmed up over the summer months bringing in the schools of mackerel.

I haven't an answer to the phenomenon that took place in August 1942, but here are the facts. We know that on the night in question there was a total eclipse of the moon. In the morning we were amazed to find the net spread out along the shore, high and dry, the anchor and mooring stone were still attached. Fish of all varieties filled every square foot, they had hit the net with such force that the net had been forced back over their bodies; usually they were held by the net just over the gills. It took a week of our spare time to remove the fish and repair the net; most of the catch was facing the same way.

So what caused it? Why did so many fish hit the net at high speed? We had often seen dolphins going up and down the channel but never had we seen them close in to the shore. We had seen a seal a number of times, its head just above the water, watching our antics. I have even thought of a miniature submarine practising at night, close in to the shore, perhaps. We had seen commandos in camouflage-coloured kayaks close in, but they would hardly drive fish into what must have been a frenzy.

Did the Germans take advantage of a moonlit night with a period of known darkness to land an agent; and don't be too quick to put this theory down as schoolboy imagination just yet.

We are left with one other possible cause that is worthy of serious consideration, the total eclipse of the moon. Were the fish disorientated by gravitation variations?

We didn't hear the sirens, the sound of aircraft, or the explosions, which is not as strange as it sounds. We often heard bumps in the night, depth charges or heavy gunfire out in the Channel, and air raids on Falmouth. We were often disturbed by the sound of aircraft too, either friend or foe, waking up and listening for a while, before pulling the bedclothes over our heads and going back to sleep.

However, the two bombs that fell that night were less than a quarter of a mile away. We ate our breakfast oblivious of the fact that windows had been broken in our garage by the blast from the two bombs.

On our way to school one or two locals were standing in the road as we approached. There it was, a large crater, the centre of which was smack in the middle of the highway. If the bomb aimer had intended – for reasons best known to himself – to cut the lower part of Restronguet Point off from the rest of England, then he had hit the bull's eye.

Of course it could be that a friendly aircraft returning from a mission had for one reason or another jettisoned their bombs, hence no sirens, but it was rumoured that several bombs had fallen into the estuary that night. We wished we had known as there could have been stunned fish out there for the taking.

We scouted around the perimeter of the crater. There was only just enough room to pass. Then up the hill to catch the bus to school. That was it really, a crater, a large hole in the road. We had all the shrapnel we wanted, the bartering rate for bomb bits was at an all time low, although shell nose cones were in big demand, as were live .303 cartridges, and leaflets dropped by the Luftwaffe.

On the way home that evening the crater had been filled in and the road reinstated. The workmen were packing up, but they informed us that a second bomb had fallen on the beach below the laundry.

A large tree had at one time fallen in the sea just a little way along the shore towards Looe Beach. It was there when we moved in, and was still there after the war when we left. This was a favourite play area for us, the tree's bark had long since gone, the wood bleached white by the sun and salt water. We often walked out along the horizontal trunk, fished from there, or sailed model boats made from cork and seagull feathers, or empty pilchard tins, the still-attached lid acting as a sail. We also used the tree as a jetty.

I don't suppose I ever knew which type of tree it was. The wood was hard, it would take day's sawing to get rings off it to make wheels for our fish cart, heating a poker red hot to burn a hole through the centre for the axle. If mum couldn't find us, we were either out in the boat or playing on the tree.

Of all places for a bomb to hit, a tree – our tree! It struck the top branches, exploded, splitting the hard wood as if it was a match. The rocks below became shingle, and yet not one single piece of shrapnel was ever found. It had exploded high up,

three hundred yards away from our house, smashing the windows in our garage, and yet as I have said we didn't hear a thing. Fresh air and exercise I suppose.

Dad bought another boat, larger than the *Swordfish*, with an inboard engine. He named it *Steep Holmer*. The engine had seen better days and so it was replaced with an almost new Coventry Victor single-cylinder job. It was a beautiful, reliable engine, despite the fact that it needed the expert's constant care. We will, in the following chapters of this book, share many adventures together aboard her, and for those reasons I will give you the once over – a crash course on boatmanship 1940s style. In those days tools, were found in a kitchen drawer, a knife became a screwdriver, wire was worth its weight in gold.

It wasn't until she was in the water that we discovered one or two problems, the most serious of which was that she leaked and had to be pumped out every day. Dad was often away and I was put in charge. Translated that meant I had to swim out to her before catching the bus to school.

I had it off to a fine art, out of bed into a swimming costume, out the front door, into the sea, pump her out, dive over the side, swim ashore, that was it, job done, Bob's your uncle! Eight minutes perhaps, longer if the sea was rough. Exhilarating it might have been, but I was not sorry when, over the winter months, she was made watertight.

She had no gearbox, just start the engine and off. Stopping was by shorting the spark plugs on the cylinder head with a piece of wire wound around a short stick, or a screwdriver. The fuel pipe was wound around the exhaust pipe, to preheat the paraffin and save petrol. The magneto had to be removed after every trip, to prevent German airmen pinching the boat and sailing her back across the Channel!

She was not fitted with a silencer, and for that reason used only in daylight hours. But enough of boats for the time being; it's harvest time at Restronguet Point, in August 1942. Our help is required!

We could hear the Fordson towing the binder a long way off. The noise of the engine, the scraping of metal on the road echoing through the lanes, to us it sounded like music. Nothing but nothing sounded so exciting at this time of the year, as the oats ripened in the sea breezes. We never ventured far away, for us the harvest took the place of bonfire nights which were then banned. There would be a gathering of 'helpers' following the tractor, boys and girls each carrying a stick, one or two on bikes some with iron hoops propelled by a nail in the end of a stick.

There wasn't any need to go looking for them, they all would hear the arriving tractor. Joe and his sister Elizabeth would be rowing across from Restronguet Weir with the sound of the engine ringing out across the water.

We were not the only ones to sense excitement in the air that day. Rabbits, lots of them, would be stamping their back legs on the ground sending out warning signals. Hidden from view, we knew they were there.

Drawn on a trailer was the binder, all folded up, with large wooden arms that would draw the standing crop on to the cutting blades.

Jack, with our help, slowly set about the task of preparing the binder, threading string through the knotter, oiling all moving parts. This Heath Robinson-looking contraption took shape, and soon it would be cutting the standing oats, wrapping string around each bundle, tying a knot and throwing each sheaf out on to the stubble in rows. That's where we took over. Each holding a sheaf we would stack them into wigwam-like stooks to dry. As we held the sheaves close to our bodies the golden straw would crackle,

As the binder came to life with a whirling, squeaking sound it was doing what it had been designed to do, although mice had bitten holes in the canvas bed, and wire held the ageing framework together. Hundreds of these implements, all over the English countryside, were gathering in the desperately-needed harvest. To us it was fun, enjoyment that would be remembered by all who were there.

Starting on the outer edges of the field the binder worked round and round the ever-decreasing squares of remaining standing grain, until stacking stooks was temporarily put to one side and, sticks at the ready, we waited for what was the exciting bit.

We could see the rabbits darting this way and that, back and forth, frightened by the clanging monster, and waiting to dodge little humans with large sticks. Finally, for them, it was decision time, stay or bolt.

Bolting for the nearest hedge, past mad shouting children waving sticks. Boys shouting girls screaming, it was now or never. Rabbits are past masters at the art of dodging, stopping dead from thirty miles per hour, turning and running in the opposite direction, leaving their pursuers flat on their faces.

In truth no rabbits were ever caught; it was a game between humans and rabbits, how happy we were, and why not! Such were the golden days spent in a field that sloped down to the sea, the fresh air mixed with the smell of tractor vaporising oil, the golden stooks of harvest drying in the summer sun. Tomorrow we would take Jack's lemonade bottles back to the shop, four pennies shared; we were rich in more ways than one

The large steam traction engine had arrived at the farm, covered in oil and grease, blackened with smoke and grime from weeks of nonstop thrashing, a living mechanical monarch dripping water and blowing steam from various parts of its anatomy; it was thrashing time.

Those of you who have seen these shining brightly coloured traction engines at steam fairs, or have looked at paintings and photographs and come to the conclusion that those were romantic carefree days, take it from me, threshing was a one off experience.

We volunteered just the once, and that was once too often.

"You can rake the chaff," (or 'douse' as it was called by the locals) said the red-faced man, with a toothless grin, passing us a wooden rake. "As the douse falls out under the thrasher, rake it out, bag it with the wooden shovel then stack the bags against the wall." And as he walked away he shouted "Go easy on the cider!" He could have saved his breath, we had been told that a dead rat was added to the brew 'to give it body'.

The traction engine gave off black smoke and steam, the pulley wheels started to rotate, the internal sieves banged up and down just inches from our heads. We bagged the chaff, ducking the

Smoke belches from a traction engine at a typical scene of thrashing during the 1940s.

main driving belt as we did so. There wasn't one part of our bodies that escaped the needle-sharp chaff; hair, nose, eyes, ears; you name it the chaff found it. Nonstop it went on, sheaths thrown in at the top, oats and chaff came out at the bottom.

Straw was loaded on to a cart then pulled away by a large black and white horse. Coal was shovelled into the furnace, black smoke belched from the funnel as we toiled all day. Our eyes were sore, throats were dry, until finally the last sheaf was thrown in.

Thank goodness, that was over, we were off, heading for the beach, shirts carried under our arms. We swam under the cool water; small fish darting here and there. Crabs scurried, small sea horses just looked, the seaweed waved; never had seawater tasted so good, we filled our mouths then spat it out. It took a hose pipe followed by a hot bath and lots of red Lifebuoy soap to remove the last of our one and only 'Day of the Thresher.'

It was just a normal Saturday in mid September, 1942, the net had been hauled, fried fish for breakfast, as it always was at weekends. Firewood had

been sawn and chopped, the *Steep Holmer* had been pumped out, all in all a quite ordinary Saturday with not a lot of excitement.

The apple pinching situation had been solved with Mr Holman agreeing to us picking up windfalls, which removed the excitement somewhat. Where before there were always apples in the larder, now we had to be asked. There was at that time also a call for rose hips and acorns, something to do with the war effort. Children gathered them and collection areas were set up. The hedges in the surrounding fields were alive with wild roses bushes and we delivered over half a hundred weight of each. Later a call went out for conkers, and we spent hours doing our bit, only to be told that due to the overwhelming response, no more were required.

Often the day would start with "what shall we do?" and always the unexpected would turn up; it wasn't that we were ever bored, far from it. But everybody had their likes and dislikes. Rounders seemed a favourite. The harvest had been gathered in, there was a field of stubble, we had a ball, and used the cricket bat given to us by PC Steer. Teams were picked; the "we bags to bat first" bit had been settled and the game was under way.

We were treated to our own superb flying display.

As one we all ducked, they came from nowhere; skimming the field, no more than twenty feet high. If we exaggerate, thirty in truth, three of them close together, Spitfires. We could smell the exhaust fumes, hear the whistling of the Merlin engines as we had never heard them before. This was the closest we had ever been to a flying machine in its natural environment, and there were three of them. In a flash they had dropped down to sea level, and were skimming the water

We were watching a superb flying display; the timing of which was spot on, as the girls were winning at rounders. Our saviours headed towards Looe Beach flying at sea level, banking left and disappearing behind the trees Then they reappeared, heading towards us, banking left again and flying in a large semi-circle, once again flying behind the trees, the three of them flying together. But when they reappeared one was missing, three had disappeared two had reappeared, and these two flew off to the north.

We were playing on stubble; all of us were wearing shoes, and as one we were off, out the gate with no time to confer. Bob grabbed his bike, his legs were going like pistons, it was everyone for themselves, no waiting. Up Restronguet Hill we ran without slackening the pace, Bob's bike ended up in the hedge.

We were all tremendously fit, rowing had built our chests, climbing rocks and trees had built leg muscles, running was second nature to us, we ran everywhere, except on Sundays or when we were smoking a Woodbine! Many times we had run this way to the shops, but never had we covered so much ground so quickly as we did that day.

Anne was a good short-distance runner and she took the lead. However we knew stamina would count and this was a race. We ran past the farm (we had perfected the art of climbing over gates, jump on the first rung, throw your body over grabbing the second and third bar, throw your legs over your head and pull with one hand and push with the other, landing, looking in the right direction, off again, no time wasted), on across the field, cutting a corner, in line now, straggled out across the field.

Farmers didn't spray fields then, in fact farmers didn't spray anything, thistles were two feet high, and we had no time to dodge them, or cow pats either. The shortest, and fastest route was a straight line. On, over another gate then back on to the road where the postman was coming down the hill on his red bicycle with a carrier on the front, smart in his blue suit with red piping down the trouser leg. He had just seen the Spitfire crash but it would be more than his job was worth to

Taken from the spot where the Spitfire ended up after ploughing down the slope, then up the incline.

leave his bicycle and mail unattended. Informing the first person he met was his only option, and we were the first.

We didn't stop or slow down, so he shouted directions over his shoulder, "Pass the Feock turning, first gate, second field down."

Pacing was over, we knew how far we had to go, and not for one moment did we stop and think of what we might find, a trapped and injured pilot, or worse. Luck was on our side, as we got to the gate Dad was cycling towards us. He must have had quite a surprise, children running towards him in line and vaulting over a gate.

"A Spitfire has crashed in the next field". We shouted. A second bicycle was thrown into the ditch and off we went together down over the field with Dad shouting "Let me go ahead just in case." Too late there it was, near the hedge, ten yards or so from the gate, tail up nose down.

The pilot was sitting on the leading edge of the wing; he said his hydraulics had packed up while on patrol over the Channel. Dad took him to the Post Office for a cuppa and to inform those who were informed in situations like this. I was left in charge, me, twelve years old in charge of a real, live, still-hot Spitfire.

The aircraft had ploughed across the field, down one side and up the other, leaving behind a trail of bits. Children were soon strewn along the furrow that had been left in the grass. Charles Gilbert had half of a propeller blade that had broken off. Among the bits of metal, twisted and shining, souvenir hunting was in full swing. But not for me, I was in charge. I had a duty to 'guard that plane'. Walking round the wing I climbed on to it taking notice of the yellow stencilling that warned "do not stand beyond this line." And then I climbed down into the open cockpit. Sitting on a utility canvas seat I couldn't see out; the pilot had sat on his parachute which gave him height, added to which he was taller than I was.

The engine was still hot, and gave off a smell of oil and petrol vapour. The structure seemed to me, utilitarian, the frame built of aluminium tubes which held the outer skin in place, giving the aircraft its beautiful shape, and yet my thoughts were that there was very little protection for the pilot. I studied each instrument, gently touching the tape-covered ring on the joy stick, noting the firing button. This was for real, not a static museum piece, this aircraft was over the Channel just under half an hour ago. I was alone with my

I had to include a PC Steer in this sketch; after all he played a major role in our lives, a policeman and a good friend.

thoughts. For as long as I could remember, I dreamed of joining the Royal Navy, but as I sat there in the cockpit I had an overwhelming desiring – I just had to fly. Working extra hard at school, I would take every opportunity that came my way to turn dreams into reality.

Voices or to be more precise, a voice, brought me back to earth, it was Police Constable Steer "Where is the pilot?" I heard him shout.

It was Saturday, half-day, work stopped at twelve o'clock and usually the local keeper of law and order could be found at the Punch Bowl and Ladle, relaxing and no doubt listening to bar gossip, picking up useful information. It would be there at the bar that he would have received the news of a downed Spitfire on his patch.

With this in mind, together with hindsight, what I did was unkind. I lifted myself up, stood on the seat and shouted, "Here!"

His face said it all, he started to speak, changed his mind, I can only guess as to his thoughts: "It's them, the apple pinching, Woodbine smoking, plague-of-my-life scallywags, and now they have got their hands on a Spitfire!"

At that precise moment reinforcements arrived in the form of Home Guard, Private Guy, holding a rifle although it's unlikely he had any ammunition. "I've come to guard the plane," he shouted.

But I had been left in charge after all, and I was only acting on Dad and the pilot's orders. "Don't stand there those cannons might go off they're loaded!" I ordered. There was an immediate response and the new arrival lifted his legs high as he walked quickly around to the back of the wing.

Then Dad came back and had a chat with the 'grown-ups'. More reinforcements from the Home Guard arrived and were put on official guard duty. The souvenir hunters were kept out – not that there was anything movable left.

On the following Monday a sixty-foot long 'Queen Mary' lorry painted in RAF colours took away our Spitfire. Dad brought home the cockpit cover which was a souvenir hunter's dream. One wet day Bob sat in a cardboard box on the kitchen table, with the cockpit cover over his head, making sounds of a Merlin engine and a machine gun. Dogfight after dogfight took place until, over the edge of the table he went, looping the loop sideways – he had 'bought it' and we had another downed pilot on our hands.

The cover was put in the cellar where it remained until the following summer when a very good use was found for it.

Chapter 7

LOW TIDE

It was autumn, soon the *Swordfish* would be brought ashore for safety and its annual paint job, but there was always time for just one more adventure.

Over on the far side of the estuary not far from St Mawes, was a grounded freighter. She had been towed there in 1940, badly damaged either by a mine or a bomb. She was about a mile and a half away, perhaps a little further, and had yet to be given the once over by ourselves. On Saturday morning, the sun was out, the sea was calm except for a slight swell, seven of us set out. John Salmon had joined the Blackburn brothers and the four of us, Anne Jean Bob and me. The milk had been fetched from the farm, the fishing jobs were done, apples gathered, lunch packed. Rules at that time were 'always stay within sight of home' which gave us plenty of scope.

Heading towards St Just in Roseland, the ebb tide would take us down towards the freighter. Rowing and singing at the top of our voices we made good progress. John Salmon was a stickler for naval procedure, no left or right for him, "port and starboard" please, and although we didn't have a compass, it was "steer south-east."

As we rounded the bow of the grounded freighter we faced a sight of utter destruction, only visible from the St Mawes side was a gaping hole large enough to take a double decker bus. From sea level to the deck was a mass of rusting twisted metal. We slowly edged nearer, the sea was calm but, as I have said, there was a slight swell.

A large sign on the deck warned KEEP OFF DANGER. "Let's go in someone suggested," most of the crew were in favour, others not too keen.

Stern-first we entered what was once the engine room, where undoubtedly men had died. Limpets, other sea life and weed had begun colonization; this was to become their habitat. The rusting metal mixed with salt water gave off fumes that could be felt in the top of the nose, not unpleasant, almost a clean disinfectant smell about it. An iron ladder that was once attached to the bulkhead hung like a clock pendulum swinging slightly in the swell. A door high above us was half open and a shaft of sunlight lit a section of iron grating and a smashed wheel valve. Above our heads, out of sight, a rope with what was probably a ship's block attached, knocked against metal, and beat in rhythm with drops of falling sea water that had been trapped by the ebbing tide.

The sounds echoed and re-echoed throughout this area of destruction, enhanced by overall silence. Not one of us said a word, the light wind funnelled up through broken steam pipes moaning softly. Below through the crystal clear water we could clearly see small fish swimming around what was once the engine, while no doubt conger eels, crabs and other larger marine species had taken up residence throughout the bilges.

In the oceans of the world, hundreds of ships lay at the bottom of the sea, viewed only by sea creatures – there were no amateur divers then – seven of us had seen nature taking back what was rightfully hers. "Let's go home," someone said, and so we did, each of us carrying their own thoughts. We never to returned; that haunting place was not a playground, it was a tomb where undoubtedly human life had ended, and marine life was beginning.

My sketch of the wrecked freighter near St Mawes.

Truro Senior Boys' School was well equipped, and the carpentry room was no exception. Each class pupil had their own bench, complete with a strong vice and a built in cupboard underneath.

I am not a carpenter, never was and never will be, however I enjoyed woodworking classes. My bench was next to my good friend Reggie James, who came from a family of carpenters and lived in Feock, opposite the school. The project in hand was a wooden stool, about eighteen inches square, and the same height. Cost of materials was four shillings, which in those days was a fair amount of money.

The woodwork master had been injured during the early days of the war; he used crutches and I think suffered considerable pain, often leaving us to get on with it, and resting in a room across the hall. We didn't take advantage of being 'left to get on with it'; everybody liked him despite having to duck on occasions when he threw a chunk of wood at one of us for not paying attention.

Now Reg and I were next to the door and we could hear his crutches on the wooden floor, which gave us fair warning to have a quick change around of the job in hand. The partly-built stools would be having Reggie's full attention, while a waterline model of HMS *Exeter* would reappear from the locker under the bench.

That model was my pride and joy, a combined effort, made from a block of red cedar driftwood. The guns were of aluminium from a crashed Spitfire, turned by an apprentice at HTP Motors in Truro, and inspected by an Air Ministry chap. The base had been made by Mr Hartnell, the flags painted by my sisters; all parts were built as near to scale as possible, and were made from recycled bits and pieces. Recycling at that time, was the norm, in fact it was a necessity.

HMS *Exeter* of the Battle of River Plate fame had recently been sunk by the Japs. Many members of her crew had lived locally and were either lost, or made prisoners of war. She meant more to me than a wooden stool; Reg had the skill, he collected cigarette cards, and I had a good supply! So far so good.

H.M.S. EXETER

A fine painting of HMS Exeter *by W. E. Broadly.*

At that time there was a craze for making 'things that went bang. At home we made carbide bombs, purchasing the ingredients from a bicycle shop adding a little water into a screw top bottle and throwing it into the sea, hoping to stun a fish or two, with very little success. Our Scout master used dynamite and a long fuse, but he didn't have any success either.

By far the most popular bomb was made from two engineering bolts held together with a nut to which a secret compound was added. Now I had to go one better, larger bolts and of course a larger nut, one and a half inches across. Stupidly I threw it into the air in the playground, the whole of Truro must have heard the bang; it's a wonder that the sirens didn't sound! The threads were stripped clean, up into the air went one big bolt and I watched in horror as it spun higher than the school. But what goes up has to come down, and there were lots of boys looking skyward. Luck was on my side – I sweat when I think about it – on the way down it ended hitting the top landing of the metal fire escape with a clang.

Later I stood in the Headmaster's room. Mr Delahunt said very little and no mention was made of the reason I was there. This experienced teacher was at the end of his long career and had been through two wars. During the Great War he had done his very best for those of his pupils who had lost someone near and dear, and no doubt there were many. 'His' children would be those who would have to rebuild an injured nation.

Now history was repeating itself. This time however was different, for many of his second-generation pupils had experienced the pointed end of hostilities, and the end was not yet in sight.

This boy standing in front of him deserved to be taught a lesson for his foolish action, a lesson that would be remembered for the rest of his life But the teacher had long since come to the conclusion that physical punishment was pointless – soon over, soon forgotten. No, he had a far better solution.

Finally he said "That will be all Harding. Oh, by the way, remember, there are more ways of killing a cat than choking it with best butter." What a funny thing to say, I had no intention of killing our cat, it kept the rabbit catcher away.

Back to the carpentry lesson. It was a special day, a dignitary was paying a visit, we proudly stood at attention, our finished stools displayed

The stool, made by Reggie James.

on the bench in front of us. Around they walked, the woodwork teacher introducing each one of us in turn. I swear that Mr Delahunt had a grin on his face. The big-wig and his escorts stopped in front of Reg and me. "That's a fine stool you have made," he said picking up mine.

"John didn't make that said the Headmaster, he is making a model ship for my office. Show Mr —," he instructed me. Out came my pride and joy, how the hell he knew it was there has remained a mystery but taking it from me he said, "Finished at last; well worth waiting for. Thank you John, top marks." So that was it, 'no butter no cat'.

From thereon the model stood on a shelf in the Headmaster's study, alongside silver cups and trophies won over the years. I had lost my pride and joy but it had found its rightful place. HMS *Exeter* was a West Country ship and the model was displayed in a West Country School.

Somewhere today there is in the West Country I hope, a fine waterline model of HMS *Exeter*, about twelve inches long, made of straight-grained red cedar wood.

But the story of the stool didn't end there; over the many years that passed since then, Mum had proudly shown off her son's carpentry skills, painted in different colours over the years, but never underneath until, as happens to us all, she had to move into a flat and no longer had room for 'my' stool.

"Take it home John," she said. For me, it was confession time.

"I didn't make it, Mum," I said.

"I know," she replied with a smile, turning it over. It's still there, written in pencil, 'R James'.

Today it seems inconceivable that in the 1940s when children up to the age of fourteen, and beyond, witnessed and understood the meaning of death, they were at the same time ignorant of 'the facts of life', a subject considered by far the largest majority of parents as taboo.

Our parents, in line with others when faced with questions of a delicate nature, had set answers.

"Where did we come from?"

"We found you under a gooseberry bush."

Or, "The cat brought you in."

But there were times when such 'stone walling' backfired on them.

One day I remember one of our chickens had about eight baby chicks, all yellow. They took refuge under the mother hen who sat down on them. I asked "How do they manage to breathe?" which Dad must have mistaken as 'breed'.

"One day you will be old enough to know, now go and get ready for tea." I was twelve years old. Mary and June who were thirteen and fourteen respectfully, were as much 'in the dark' as their younger brothers and sisters.

Mum had a very good friend, a Mrs Kessell who periodically came for afternoon tea; her visits were very special, held in the lounge with best china and all the trimmings. We liked her very much, she smelt of talcum powder and watched us over the top of her spectacles. Having no children of her own we were spoilt, and were given sixpence each if we sang or recited for her. Dressed in clean cloths, polished shoes, hair brushed, we took it in turns, youngest first.

Bob stood on a chair, looking for all the world a saint. His blue eyes sparkling, face scrubbed pink he started singing 'When I'm cleaning windows':

"There's hair on this
And there's hair on that,
Hair on every pussy cat,
But I know where there's more than that,
When I'm cleaning windows."

I cannot describe the look on Mum's face, her boy, her pet. I knew that I was about to get the blame, act quick I thought, after all my friends and I often went in to the museum, just to get a peek at a large painting of a nude lady. I was the eldest here, it was my duty to save our visitor's blushes, and our sixpences were at risk.

"That's rude;" I shouted. "Bob has sung the rude version."

Mum's relief showed, "Yes he has, he is a naughty boy. You sing the correct one dear."

I didn't stand on the chair, luck was on my side, I was between the ladies and the open door.

I held my head up, every word was clear, I was giving it my all:

"Now Mrs brown she lives next door
She's having babies by the score,
When I get in she'll have some more
When I'm cleaning windows."

I think that's about as far as I got, Mum had lost her special voice, for special people, and I most certainly at that moment was not special. Mrs Kessell just stared ahead.

"Go to your bed at once," Mum ordered, "your Father will deal with you when he gets home. That's where my Bobby gets it from, you, you naughty boy."

Bob had sung the rude version and he had sixpence, I had sung the clean version and was given the stinging nettle treatment!

Ted had a pet rabbit, a beautiful blue one, I wanted a rabbit. Now Aunty Lil's husband was a prisoner of war so she moved in with her sister, Mrs Blackburn. We asked Lil if Ted's rabbit could have babies. "It will have to be crossed" she said, wishing to change the subject.

But I wanted a rabbit and I wasn't going to be brushed off, "What do you mean crossed?"

Ted's Mum was standing by the wall saying nothing, just smiling. She must have been thinking "get out of that if you can."

Lil was a Londoner through and through, a quick thinker, "It has to have a cross on its back," Lil said walking away. "Is that the time, I must go."

Hard to believe two boys aged twelve and thirteen could be so naive but we did just that. Mr Hartnell found an almost empty tin of white paint, and with a stick we painted a cross on the buck rabbit's back, then waited, and waited.

Mum had not been too well, having to rest a lot. Dorothy was engaged to help out, cooking, washing and so on. We all loved her, not just because of her 'hot pots', but because she laughed a lot, and was particularly close to my elder sisters. I later learnt that she had 'taken them under her wing' regarding painting crosses on rabbits.

One day Dorothy shouted to us as we were just offshore in the boat, "Go and meet your Dad off the bus, tell him to hurry home, the doctor's here."

We walked at a fast pace down the hill, Dad and I, running and walking at the same time. It was Thursday, the day of the 'Knockout' comic. It was only an innocent remark, I was just making conversation, so to speak, when I said, "Did you get the comic today?"

Dad lost his cool, I was given a lecture, "Don't you think that I have nothing better to do than go shopping for a damn comic. Grow up for goodness sake."

And so we hurried on down the hill, Dad with his thoughts, and me feeling a little peeved; after all he was always the first to read the comic while we had to wait. Now, when I look back to those times, it somehow seems that we had been brushed by the wings of death, having to come to terms with the loss of a friend, having to watch men die, and yet we were not mature enough to understand the creation of life.

After tea we were told by Mary and June to "go out and play." This in real terms meant digging early potatoes, chopping wood, and of course setting the net. To be fair we never distinguished between chores and play, we treated them just the same.

Dad called to us, he was standing outside the kitchen door, chest out shoulders back, grinning from ear to ear. We wondered what he was about to say, perhaps the war was over, or he had found the comic in his pocket. "My Dears I have something to tell you all, wonderful news, you have a little sister. We are calling her Margaret. Now

have a good wash and change into clean clothes then you can see her, one at a time."

A short while ago I stood on the very spot in the playground of Truro Senior Boys' School, in the shadow of the cathedral, where I had once changed from a naive child to worldly wise teenager. I knew where to find my friend Stinker Hughes that morning, we were good friends and sat together in class. He was a year older than the rest of us, and had taught me to play chess. It's strange how children have their own area of the playground, their patch. Yes he was there, having finished his paper round, and was catching up on breakfast. "I have a baby sister." I said, but the answer I received was not the one expected. He said in a firm tone, "Your father has been at it again, the dirty devil."

I raised my voice in anger "It was nothing to do with him he wasn't there, I met him off the bus."

Stinker stopped eating his bread and jam and ran around the playground telling everyone what Harding had said, but, much to his astonishment very few boys understood what all the fuss was about, a very large percentage in fact were as naive as Harding was.

I give Stinker full marks, he took it upon himself to educate the ignorant, and so during morning and afternoon break times he gave a lecture on the subject while standing on a lavatory seat. There were those who listened and those who laughed at Stinker's human biology lectures. However it was agreed by all that he had enlightened us, even though he was at times wide of the mark.

It took many years for me to forgive him for insisting that one should never choose a partner taller than one's self. I was five foot one and a half at the time; it narrowed the field somewhat.

Chapter 8

THE TURNING TIDE

From the middle of 1943 a steady influx of US ships and personnel arrived in the South of England. Their presence was more noticeable on the roads, Jeeps and six-wheel-drive lorries seemed to be everywhere, often travelling at high speed through the narrow country lanes. Drivers not yet accustomed to driving on the left-hand side of the road, but not at home on the right, drove in the middle!

I liked to sit next to the bus driver, watch him pull the long gear lever across the box, pause halfway, rev the engine, then feel the selected gear before engaging. We were climbing up the long hill towards Playing Place in the grey utility Bedford which had wooden seats – not unlike a lighter version of a park bench.

We were on one of the few straight sections of the road, when heading towards us in the centre of the road was a six-wheel lorry towing an empty low-loading trailer, possibly used for transporting tanks. The bus driver slowed down, the American driver at the last moment moved over to the right-hand side of the road, misjudged the width and the trailer went up the bank and rolled completely over right into our path.

For the Yanks there was no panic, it was just one of those things. About twenty or so GIs jumped out of a following truck, lifted the trailer on to its side, leaned it on the bank and waved us on.

That was the way things were at that time with the newly arrived American army, and navy – an outward portrayal of nonchalance with no arm waving, shouting, or waiting for orders. Outwardly at least, the chain of command was less apparent. Over the next twelve months we would witness many such incidents; however at the same time we were to get an insight into their thoughts, fears, and dreams.

And so as the year progressed and preparations for the invasion gathered momentum we were to have a ringside seat. As children there were very

few restrictions and we had a unique opportunity to be 'in on the action', young enough not to be considered a security risk, and yet old enough to understand, and remember. The tide of war had turned.

Due to the build up of shipping in the area beachcombing took on a new dimension; there was to be no shortage of firewood. The wooden boxes and crates we gathered were sawn and chopped. We tasted coffee for the first time when small waterproof sachets, about the size of a tea bag, were washed in. Later there would be 'K' Rations which contained everything from chocolate to hard biscuits, and tins of soup with candle-like heating facility built through the centre; just light the wick stand back, hey-presto! warm soup.

One problem we had, and had no control over, was the prevailing wind which blew from the west. This resulted in most of the flotsam ending up on the St Just in Roseland side of the estuary, where, as far as we knew, there were no beach-combers, and so we made the occasional crossing in the *Swordfish*.

Mostly these trips were routine, just row one way, sail the other, and drop a fishing line over the side; a pleasant day out. However one such trip did not go according to plan.

The wind was light from the north-east, the sunrise had been pink, nothing more. As there were no weather forecasts during the war, we read the sky, wind direction and so on; we knew that in warm weather the difference in land and sea temperatures, brought an increase in wind speeds during the afternoon.

We had an all-boy crew that day, the girls were babysitting. Setting out in high spirits we headed for an area we had visited many time before. Beating time with the oars we sang one of our favourites, 'What shall we do with the drunken sailor', we hadn't a care in the world.

The beach was littered with timber, rope, half a lifebelt; I could not begin to remember everything, but the most rewarding for us were about eight oak barrels, not the standard size but about three feet in length, painted grey. There were a quite a few tins of ship's biscuits one of which we opened on the beach. I cannot remember how we opened them, most likely a screw top, or a key, as there would have to have been a simple way in order that they could be opened in a ship's lifeboat, where most likely they had come from. The biscuits were brown in colour, hard and almost impossible to bite, and to tell the truth not designed to be enjoyed. However they were intended to sustain life, a topic at that time we didn't dwell on. Although we didn't like them, after crushing them, the chickens did.

We beached the *Swordfish*, and as the tide was ebbing soon she would be high and dry. Loading her was no problem, and load her we did. There was no room to sit and row and it was a case of sitting in the bilges. With the wind and tide in our favour we would sail on the return trip.

It would be a little while before the boat would refloat and a bonfire was suggested. So below high water mark, where the incoming tide would douse the fire before blackout time, we piled up everything that would burn. This was five years' worth of bonfire nights rolled into one! Rocks cracked and seaweed melted under the heat of the fire, and the black smoke could have been seen for miles around. The more it burnt the more we piled on; so engaged were we that the ever increasing strength of the wind went unnoticed. Eventually the tide came in, and with the boat, fully laden we 'floated off'. All aboard, sail hoisted, and we were off.

For the first half mile or so things went well. However as we moved out into the estuary, away from the lee shore, we began to feel the effect of the freshening wind. There was no turning back; we had got ourselves into this situation and we had to see it through. With the wind gaining in velocity by the minute, the sea was becoming more choppy as a result.

We were in trouble on two counts one, there was a real danger of us ending up having to swim, and second, for the first time we noticed that we were plastered in oil.

The removable platform that had been fitted was now put to good use. Standing on it gave greater leverage on the steering oar, although for the first time it took two of us at the helm, the barrage balloon sail was pulling hard. Jettisoning our cargo was an option, however if we ended up in the briny, and there was a strong possibility of that, barrels could be used for buoyancy.

The *Swordfish* did everything but take off, yawing in the following sea. Taking down the sail would be risky as it would entail standing up. Then we noticed a high-powered motorboat heading towards us from Restronguet Creek. She passed just astern, dipping her bow into the sea and leaving behind a cloud of spray. Her skipper stepped out of the cabin and waved to us. The fact that we were oily-faced kids peeping over the gunnels of a boat with a barrage balloon sail, and he was in a luxury motor cruiser, made not the slightest difference. All sailors are equal when at sea, and so he gave us the traditional wave.

We were fast heading for the shore under our house. There was continuous bailing of the bilges with a large tin, and with a hundred yards to go it was decision time. All the crew would have to move back to the stern and at the same time the sail would be 'let go' and we would run her ashore.

It didn't go exactly to plan. When everyone moved aft to lift the bow, the water in the bottom of the boat ran back too and the stern went under water. Slowly we began to sink but just fifty feet from the shore I was deprived of giving the order "abandon ship" as the swabs had already jumped overboard, and anyway we didn't abandon her, she abandoned us.

I will do my best to describe the scene of oil-covered, very wet adventurers sitting on the seaweed-covered shore, spitting out oily-tasting sea water. Salvaged jetsam became flotsam once more, as Ted and I went aboard the sad looking *Swordfish* with buckets, baling like mad and refloated her.

We removed the worst of the oil from our skin with paraffin-soaked rags, then soap and hot water in a tin bath in the garden with a scrubbing brush and red carbolic soap. We scrubbed each other until finally we were ready for a hot bath.

The barrels were sold to a neighbour, who paid us one pound and twelve shillings for them, my best trousers became school trousers, school trousers became play trousers, play trousers went into the Cornish range, and I had one shilling and three pence change – and six months clothing coupons lost.

It took the best part of the next day to bring the *Swordfish* back to being 'ship shape and Bristol fashion.'

As summer changed into autumn in 1943, crude oil on the beaches of Cornwall became a problem. The fishing season finished early, the boats were taken out of the water and the shore area was a 'no go' zone. Nature fought back and layers of the tar-like substance solidified and peeled off before floating away. However, for fifty or more years the rocks were stained black below the high-water mark, and today in areas away from the open sea, where over the years large waves have washed the rocks clean, the natural grey-coloured shore is still tinged black, a fading reminder of the Battle of the Atlantic.

By now the harvest had been gathered and the fields ploughed. There was not a lot of action on the war front, a lull before the storm so to speak. From our windows we could see convoys of ships heading up the English Channel. It took hours from the first sighting of the convoy until we saw the stragglers pass St Antony light. There is little doubt that on board many of those ships were American service personnel getting their first glimpse of England.

Our baby sister Margaret was growing fast, and we would often take her out into the garden and keep an eye on her as we tended the vegetable patch or sawed firewood. But there was a problem, she wanted to see what her elder brothers and sister were getting up to – and Bob had the answer.

On the beachcombing heap (the 'this will come in handy one day' pile), was a roll of what must have been camouflage netting. We made a cradle with it around the Spitfire canopy, and hanging it upside down from 'our tree' we placed her blankets in it. She was safe, warm, and most importantly, she could see out, and we could see in.

It was the last day of 1943. Tonight would be New Year's eve, there would be no fireworks, but perhaps the ships in Falmouth would blow their whistles and there would be the 'Happy New Year' wishes. But we would be sound asleep by then.

Little did we know it then but 1944 would be the most memorable year in our childhood. Even so, 1943 still had one last memory hidden up her sleeve.

About mid morning, that winter's day, we were playing draughts on the kitchen table. Out on the water the oyster boats were sailing back and forth, when there was a low vibration, gradually increasing in its intensity. Crockery started to rattle in the cupboard.

We were out the back door and into the garden in a flash. The sky was full of aircraft, from the King Harry area and beyond to the north, to St Mawes in the south were hundreds of bomber aircraft. This was our first sighting of American planes, instantly recognised as B17 Flying Fortresses; and they were so low we could easily see the aircrew as we waved.

For those living on the eastern side of England, this would have been almost a daily sight, however, for us it was a one off. We were ecstatic, every one shouting and pointing, waving and looking one way then the other. We could smell aviation fuel, and see the painted emblems on the noses of the aircraft, the letter 'J' on the tail and the white star on the fuselages. Wing tip to wing tip they came and wing tip to wing tip they disappeared over the trees at Mylor.

The adrenalin flowed in our veins as we related over and over our individual recollections, "Did you see them wave?"

"I did." "So did I!"

It could have been two hours later, perhaps longer, I cannot remember, when our euphoria turned to horror.

They came back, those same aircraft, some higher others lower, the sound of their engines no longer in harmony. We didn't have time to notice the aircrew; there was no waving, no shouting, we just stood there looking at the scars of battle, ribs clearly showing where once was aluminium. Some had one engine stopped, others two, those with no visible damage flew close to those who were struggling, giving their colleges moral support. Above us were American airmen who had been in battle just an hour before.

One of the badly damaged B17s changed direction suddenly, we never heard if it had forced landed shortly after passing over.

Thanks are due to my friend Graham J Lewis, an aeronautical historian, for the following information.

On 31 December 1943, B17 42-3093, code TU-K named 'Nobodys Darling', force landed at

The author's panoramic sketch recalling the incident of the American bombers. Below left: The cap badge of a USAAF pilot. Below right: B17 Flying Fortresses.

Burnham-on-Sea, less than half a mile away from the house where, thirteen years before, I was born.

The crew escaped uninjured. The aircraft had taken off from Polebrook, their target the U-boat pens at Bordeaux-Merignac France.

My sister Mary had a friend Eric, a naval Petty Officer, who was a coordinator between the Royal Navy and the US Navy. On occasions, after tea, we would row him back to the cove under Trelissick where he was stationed. As Eric was dressed in his naval uniform, and he was rowing, we passed close in to the shore at Turnaware.

A jetty was being constructed out into the estuary where LSTs would later in the year, take on board US troops. Further up the River Fal at Tolverne – unknown to us at that time – concrete slipways and a road were also being built. Here tanks, lorries and heavy equipment would be loaded.

LST's (Landing Ship, Tank) on arrival from the United States carried landing craft on their decks and were brought to this area. Although we never saw the unloading operation, Dennis Julian, one of our friends who lived at King Harry, said that the LSTs were listed over to about 45 degrees, and the landing craft just slid into the water with an almighty splash. I often wish that I had seen this taking place, but our boundary in the *Swordfish* was Turnaware, which was understandable as the area beyond that was a hive of military activity.

Aboard the *Steep Holmer* (which no longer leaked), Dad would often take us to Falmouth, passing close to ships of all sizes and designs, from naval destroyers to large merchant vessels.

On one such trip we had an escort; four or five large two-man kayaks were making their way up river. Although we motored alongside them for some distance, the occupants dressed in camouflage gear and wearing woolly hats ignored us, war was on their minds, and they were deadly serious.

It was a Saturday morning; there had been a strong north-easterly wind blowing overnight, and as we hadn't been beachcombing for some time due to the oil (which had now dispersed over the winter months), we set off along the shore. Almost at once we were met with railway sleepers, lots of them. Where they came from would be anyone's guess, in all probability from the landing stage at Turnaware Point. It's impossible to recall now how many there were, the general opinion from those who were there was between thirty and forty.

What could we do, the boats were out of the water, and if we had gone across to where the landing stage was being constructed and reported what we had found, in all probability no action would have been taken. However if the boats *had* been in the water we would have 'done the right thing', if for no other reason than to get a close up shufti of what was going on.

So as far as the sleepers were concerned it was 'finder's keepers' and a large scale salvage operation was put in place. At low tide there is a shingle beach along the shore; the sleepers were rolled into the water, a rope was fastened on one end, and then by paddling and towing, one by one they were brought home.

We built a ramp out of the sleepers and slid each one up the cliff, until; there was enough firewood for the inhabitants of Restronguet Point to last until peace returned. And, as we will see, the railway sleepers were put to good use in another ways too.

Mooring buoys had been laid off the deepwater channel, from the shore off St Mawes along the coast under the St Just in Roseland peninsula, then across the estuary, ending about half a mile off Restronguet.

LSTs would moor facing up-channel on arrival, waiting their turn to move up river where they loaded with tanks and other equipment. On returning they would face down-channel, in preparation for taking part in exercises, and later, the real thing.

There was a lot of coming and going, as many as twenty-five ships could be there at any given time, this number increasing considerably during late May and early June.

Small boat activity carried on without interference; we sailed, fished, and generally went about doing the things that we had always done.

On calm days, or when the wind was from the east, tannoy announcements from the moored vessels echoed across the water, and American music of the day would be played over and over again. My favourite was Glen Miller and his band, right now as I type this I am playing one of his disc's, not only for my enjoyment, but also for atmosphere, stimulating the memory. Music on the radio then was mainly for the older generation; however the sounds coming from the ships appealed to the young ones, especially the girls.

It was about seven thirty in the evening – double summer time – when 'it' paid its first of many visits. We were in bed when the sirens at Falmouth sounded, followed by others in the area. Before the wailing sound had reached its third climbing note we were out of the front door, the four of us, Anne, Jean, Bob and I. We immediately recognized the 'hunting' sound of a German bomber's engines, and there it was flying low over St Just in Roseland, heading up river. It disap-

A Junkers 88, similar to the aircraft that flew over St Just in Roseland.

peared from view, heading north, only to reappear over Trelissick, very low, down over the large field towards the estuary, and skimming the sea it banked and headed towards us.

There was a low wall at the side of the house and we ran behind it, looking over the top. We watched as the aircraft passed in front of the house out of our sight, then ran to the other side and watched as it flew off over Greatwood House at Mylor, on the far side of the creek.

Mum, Dad, and our older sisters had a better view looking out of the kitchen window. It repeated its flight path exactly, before flying off out to sea.

About two weeks later, it could have been longer, the Junkers 88 returned, twice it circled, following the same route as before. Two or three weeks later it made another visit, each time, as the days became longer, later in the evening, always appearing about sunset. Mum and Dad said that the pilot waved to them as it passed by at sea level, the height of the aircraft and the kitchen window being the same.

Who was he and what was the purpose of his daredevil sorties?

Rumours were rife, after all, never once was a bomb dropped, or cannon fired, and he was too low for photographic reconnaissance.

Mr Polglaze thought that the pilot had been a yachtsman before the war, had fond memories of the area, and returning from a bombing raid, diverted to the area he loved. But then Mr Polglaze would say that, he always saw the best in everything and everybody.

Our thoughts were that he was dropping supplies for a German agent camping out in the woods near the King Harry reaches. The Home guard, with loaded rifles, set up an ambush, while farmers had shotguns handy.

We waited to see if the pilot would wave to us, without success. However we were, in the not too distance future, to get our moments of excitement, and our German 'friends' in the Junkers would take a leading role.

Mary and June were returning from King Harry after a visit to see Eric. They had passed Trelissick House and were taking a short cut across a field where they would rejoin the road to Feock, here they spotted a man on the far side of a copse. As they watched he moved a short distance, then took a pair of binoculars out from under his coat, and slowly scanned the estuary.

At Pill Creek a couple who had, allegedly, lived in Germany before the war. Their house was a short distance away from where my sisters had seen the suspicious looking character.

The girls hurried home and told Dad what they had seen, and he in turn got on his motor bike and headed off into the yonder. The 'spy' incident was not mentioned again, at least for a week or so.

I recall that at the time 'spy' stories were rife; no doubt in the Punch Bowl and Ladle and the Pandora Inn, strangers were given the once over.

An amateur sleuth following up a hunch near Veryan was himself arrested and spent a night locked up in the local police house. Everyone had a theory and we had ours, not that we knew who the spy was, or for that matter where he lived but we were certain that a spy existed, although our many searches in the area where we suspected he was camped ended empty handed.

Way back in the days when delivery men whistled and ladies never smoked in public, boys climbed trees; the higher the tree the happier we were. Fir trees were my favourite the smell of the sap, the wind playing tunes as it whistled through the needles.

Often I sat astride a branch sixty or more feet up, alone, reading a book. I cannot remember where I read the following poem, it was many years ago:

I went for a walk,
I climbed a tree; I climbed to the top,
And I'm sixty three.
I tore my coat, Bruised my knee,
And was just a little late getting home for tea.
All that was said was "did anyone see,
What would they have thought of you, climbing
    a tree
And of course they were right
And of course I'd agree, but
I climbed that tree because
I wanted to see if,
Climbing a tree meant the same to me,
As it did to the boy I used to be.
Green, green swaying in the top of a tree,
How brave, how exploring what miles I can see.
And I climbed it because when I'm seventy three
I will still have a ten year memory, of,
Green, Green, swaying in the top of a tree.
But, one doesn't explain these things,
Not at tea.

My thanks to the unknown author.

There was a fir tree at the bottom of the garden at Steep Holm, just on the edge of the shore. Thirty feet in height perhaps, we placed planks across from one branch to another; not a tree house, just a bench where we sat looking out over the water. A large rope swung from a branch and we could run grab it and swing out over the beach, and like monkeys we would pull ourselves up to the bench hand-over-hand. The tree was our private, out of earshot, meeting place. Plans were made there; we had a view over 'our territory' which was becoming more crowded by the day.

Sitting on the bench up the tree that morning, looking out over the estuary, chatting about this and that, the LSTs were lying at anchor the music playing from their tannoys drifting across the water. Mum was hanging out the washing – she always seemed to be hanging out the washing – while a Liberty Ship was slowly making its way up channel near St Just in Roseland. A pair of tugs fore and aft were pulling her this way and that.

The vessel was painted in a light brown colour, and she was lying low in the water. Suddenly a loud high-pitched screaming sound filled the air, and very low over the fields on the opposite side of the estuary three aircraft appeared, one behind the other. They pounced on the freighter just over a mile away. Machine guns rattled, and Joe Woolcock a school friend who was on his first, and last, visit to the 'front line', slid down the rope and ran. He later told us that he didn't stop running until he was home, two miles away. I shouted to Mum, "Get in quick they are Focke-Wulf 190s" – she proudly repeated those words to all in sundry for some time after.

One after the other the German aircraft dived at the ship dropping one bomb each, then headed out over the water towards us before banking to their left. Anti-aircraft cannons on the LSTs and near St Mawes opened up; plumes of water from the three bombs lifted into the air around the ship – three near misses, thank goodness. The whole

The author's sketch of the attack as seen from 'our tree', made from memory.

The author's Focke-Wulf 190 recognition model.

incident lasted only two or three minutes then silence, they were gone, disappearing low over the sea as fast as they came.

Once again rumours were rife: 'one crew member had been killed', 'one of the aircraft had been hit', but, most disturbing of all, 'she was loaded with ammunition destined for the invasion. If so, and if one of those bombs had hit, well, the outcome does not bear thinking about'!

During wartime the way things were is the way they are, there were no 'ifs'. Having said that and looking back, one cannot help wondering what would have happened if one of the three bombs had hit the ship. There could have been one of the largest explosions in Europe during the Second World War. The resulting catastrophic destruction would have been widespread, not to mention the ships moored nearby, destined for the beaches of Normandy.

Eric came to see us that evening, he listened a lot and said little, he didn't answer our main question, "How did the German aircraft know that ship was there? They came over the hill right above it, and without having to veer left or right just pounced. Coincidence perhaps, luck maybe, or were they tipped off, and if so, by whom? From Trelissick there is an uninterrupted view of that area.

Three days later we had an invitation to look over an LST moored at King Harry, and have tea with the American skipper – Ted, Terry, Bob and me.

We were picked up, all dressed for the occasion, at the King Harry slipway by a naval pinnace. The hospitality we received from the ship's crew was first class. There was a relaxed atmosphere between ranks; engineers showed us the engine room, officers the bridge, nothing was hidden from us. However one memory stands out above the rest, I have often pictured the scene in my mind; it was the hold, empty then, hollow, large, and our voices echoed, there was little to see, but lots over the years to think about. It would be here that tanks and equipment would be stowed, men would sleep, and wait while crossing the channel. The vision of the iron ladder attached to the bulkhead, up which fully-equipped fighting men would have to climb, fast in an emergency, was a haunting thought. Was this one of the LSTs that would see action before the invasion?

We sat in the mess, before us was a spread the likes of which we hadn't seen for a long time. The conversation was jovial, crew members came and

Famous for the 'hit and run' raids, Focke-Wulf 190s appeared many times over the West Country.

A US navy clock from World War 2.

Tanks and equipment being loaded on to an LST. It was on board one of these ships the author had tea in the officers' mess, and was given VIP treatment.

went, joining in; they were enjoying our company equally as much as we enjoyed theirs. Then almost unnoticed, we were alone just the four of us, plus Eric, the skipper and two other officers. The topic of the attack on the freighter came and went, the Junkers aircraft was casually mentioned (several times), along with the London and Plymouth blitzes. All this and more, and while we answered we ate the spread before us, enjoying both.

Our first visit aboard a 'ship of war' was nothing more than that, a visit. However Eric knew of the spy sighting, we had told him of our suspicions, of the possible connection between the two events, and it was just possible that they were building an overall picture . We were living, in the best possible vantage point, apart from the woods near Trelissick House.

Two days later, Mr Polglaze told us that a US staff car and two jeeps had parked in our gateway while top brass had walked up and down the road.

On 8 March 1944, Margaret's first birthday, we arrived home from school and there they were, GIs, lots of them, taking up an area from our gate down the road for 200 yards. On 'our patch' with no prior notification! Tents, water carts, boxes large and small, two guns (one a large anti aircraft type, the other a four-barrelled cannon) along with much more that had been unloaded.

A radio mast had already been erected, tents were in place, and a large stack of shells were beside, and on, the road. Yanks were everywhere, some with tin hats on, others with peak caps or woolly hats; they were here to stay and meant business, so we left them to it.

The next four months would see a dramatic change in our lives, fishing would continue harvesting would be confined to the field above our house; we would form friendships that in reality would last for a short while, but in our thoughts have stood the test of time.

We got off to a bad start with Anglo-American relations; ignorance in the 'way of things' that were taken as normal in their homeland caused the first upset. At the top of our drive there was,

A rough sketch of the gun site, here a little 'artistic licence' has been used; the site has been moved down the road 100 yards.

and still is, a turning place, an area off the road which at that time was overgrown with brambles.

This area had been cleared and a tent erected, it was here that the black American GIs lived, some 200 yards away from their white counterparts.

Remember that it was only just a couple of weeks before I had seen a black man for the first time; he was standing in Lemon Street, Truro, looking very smart in his 'best' uniform. We were fascinated by our new neighbours, tall with broad shoulders, of African descent, their white teeth shone, bright eyes looking sad.

It couldn't have been easy for them under-standing us; equally we didn't understand their deep Southern ascent. Mum suggested that we should take them a slice of boiled cake she had made for Margaret's birthday. We had difficulty persuading them to accept but perseverance paid off. While we were doing this two white Americans passed by.

Later we were having tea and there was a knock at the door. Dad answered and we could hear voices, before Dad returned with a sergeant and one of his men. "These gentlemen would rather that you didn't associate with the chaps at the top of the drive." Dad said.

"I suggested that they take some boiled cake, we meant no harm," Mum explained.

The sergeant was polite but firm, they are here to help with the digging, erecting of tents and so on, tomorrow they will move on.

"Well if that's the case there is no problem," Dad retorted. "After tea the boys and I will be out in the boat, tomorrow they will be in school when your colleagues leave." Dad was at his best, he was in his element, "Let's have a look," he continued, taking the tin, "it seems that they didn't eat all the cake." Offering the tin he said, "Do have a slice of the wife's boiled cake, made without fat which is on ration".

The Americans took a slice of cake each, congratulating Mum on her baking. But this would not be their last visit.

We didn't see the black GI's again with their sad eyes that never met ours, however that same evening we were sitting on the stairs dressed in our pyjamas when we heard singing in the distance, deep sounds, more of a chant, a rhythm, the like of which we hadn't heard before. In our slippers we opened the front door and the four of us quietly walked up to the top of the drive. Sitting under the wall out of sight we listened. We couldn't help being moved by their spiritual chanting, their version of a hymn perhaps. A harmonica was softly playing in the background; there were no lights and in the dusk they were alone with their thoughts. It was getting cold as the air moved in from the sea; we walked back down the drive and went to bed.

In the morning they were gone.

The second upset took us by surprise. We had for the past three years walked across the fields to see our friends the Blackburn's; they were to all intents and purposes our fields. We had helped with the ploughing and harvest, caught rabbits there, nothing had prepared us for what was about to happen.

Against the top hedge a latrine had been dug, it's true that we came across it at an inopportune moment – embarrassment all round – and all hell broke loose. We thought our end had come and we ran, waiting for the sound of gunfire.

Once again a deputation arrived on our doorstep, a Yank sergeant and his sidekick. We expected the worse, we had briefed our parents, they were ready – no doubt Dad was mulling over in his mind what to say, we waited. "Would you mind Sir, if we came in and had a talk." They couldn't have been nicer, we all sat down, names were exchanged rules agreed, bus times, ferry services, nearest English pubs and so on. The cake tin was handed around. The truce lasted for one day.

We were on our way down the road, Bob and I – the short cut across the fields had been put out of bounds – and as we neared the camp we could see a lot of activity. Shells for one of the guns had been stacked at the side of the road, a chain gang was busy, each passing one to the man next to him, and they were being restacked near the gun.

The road was blocked and there was nothing for it but to wait, which we did, perhaps six feet or so away. The men were working to a rhythm every shell passed at the same time "up-two-three-four, up-two-three-four". A sergeant was overseeing the operation, we faced each other, he on one side of the chain we the other.

It happened in a split second, the GI just in front of us, lost his grip with his left hand, the shell dropped, pointing straight down; a juggling effort to regain control failed. It began to fall nose first, the sergeant dived arms outstretched and caught it at road level, pulled it into his body and lay on top of it. About eight GIs, each holding a shell (except one!), a sergeant, and two boys just stood there in amazement. It had all happened so quickly.

What happened next was a natural reaction; relief, shock, anger, and other emotions welled up inside the sergeant and he exploded in anger, and we were in the firing line. The things he said have long since been forgotten, but his swift action that day I will always remember.

We returned up the road and Bob and I sat on our gate looking out at the view, this nine year old brother of mine, who had experienced more than his fair share of near misses in his short life. However the past had taught us not to dwell on such things.

The voice behind us was the sergeant's, "Sorry about that," he said leaning against the gate, blood still showing on his chin and hands. "Why don't you come and have a look at the outfit?"

Bob asked if Ted and Terry could have a look too and soon all four of us were being given a hands-on tour. A rangefinder with powerful optics, a bazooka, a large six-inch anti-aircraft gun, and last but not least the four-barrel cannon. We each in turn, sat in the control seat and put it through its paces, looking through the sights. It was very responsive, up and down, left or right, the Junkers 88 would not stand a chance now, or would it?.

For the next three months the American gun crew became part of the community, mixing in well. We arranged to take their leftover food scraps when Dad bought a pig, 'Percy', and made him a sty from railway sleepers. Percy was fed on the very best, the likes of which we hadn't seen for some time. The GIs took over feeding him during school time.

Our friendship with the Americans grew and yet we never outstayed our welcome; we stuck rigidly to the ground rules that had been agreed, never once did we visit them at 'chow' time, although legend has it that boys would ask "have you any gum chum?", we didn't, and, I can never recall hearing school friends use that expression.

Having said that, there were are two occasions, both involving chewing gum, that are worth recording. The first happened on my way home from school. I often cycled the five miles to Truro, for not only did it save money, it also meant that I would be home early, not having to wait for the bus. There is a long winding hill, about one and a half miles long, ending at Playing Place, not steep enough to get off and walk, yet hard going peddling.

As was common practice then for cyclists to grab hold of the back of a slow-moving lorry, and just freewheel. Boys did it, men did it, and it was not uncommon to see a lady 'having a tow'. Remember that convoys of army lorries travelled at about ten miles per hour.

That particular day the chosen six-wheel drive US lorry was full of black GIs. It was part of a convoy, which had come down over the hill from Truro, passing under the railway bridge before it started its climb. It was making heavy weather and I could hear it behind me going down through down through the gears. Just the job, I thought, and as it passed I grabbed the tailboard much to the amusement of its passengers.

A packet of chewing gum went over my head and landed in the road behind. I stopped, threw the bike down, ran back, retrieved the packet and into my pocket it went. Then back on the bike, a quick burst of peddle power, I caught up with the lorry and held on.

It became a game, the GI's trying to get me to lose my free lift, while I was determined not to lose the gum or the lift. Next, two packets were thrown; the driver must have seen me in his mirror and took my side, reducing speed, and so the game continued until my pockets were full. Then they cheated; a small cardboard box with a few packets of gum in it went high into the air, landing and spilling its contents on to the road. The following lorries stopped, GIs got out and helped gather the packets. The victors carried on, laughing and waving as I stuffed the gum down the inside of my shirt.

About a week later I was walking across Lemon Quay. It was midday and I had been to see if the stone barges were in. The area was a hive of activity, barges were alongside unloading prefabricated sections of pontoons that would carry tanks and equipment ashore from ships lying off the shores of Normandy. Of course we didn't know that at the time. All we did know was that these sections were being transported to Malpas for assembly.

Coming towards me was a tall black GI and as he got nearer he stretched his arms out, then in a loud voice shouted, "No, I haven't any gum, always you ask for gum!"

I hadn't said a word but I put my hand into my pocket, took out a packet of gum and held it out, "Have mine," I said. "Please take it."

He looked nervously around and then down at this white boy offering a GI gum, then he walked away on towards the quay. I trotted beside him pleading "please take it," and so he did, without saying a word, just a smile and a nod.

Throughout the spring months we spent many memorable evenings at the gun site; no longer did they look upon us as children, and we addressed them by their first names, which was almost unheard of in those days. There was one exception; one of them was a Senator back home in the USA and he was always referred to as such by his fellow countrymen and ourselves. During one of our get-together's he explained all about American politics. The truth was we found it all confusing; at that time we were not even familiar with English politics, but we listened and we never forgot that we had befriended a GI who one day, could be the President of The United States of America.

I still believe they were telling the truth, despite the fact that so many of Mary and June's American boyfriends claimed to be Bob Hope's cousins; the comedian must have had a very large family.

We knew very little about their homeland. I had only been to the pictures three times, but we built up a mental picture of life across the Atlantic. The pride of all schoolboys at that time was the RMS *Queen Mary*, but as hard as we tried we never found out if they had 'come over' on her. They confided that they had landed at Southampton, and were shocked at the damaged caused by the Blitz, but that's as far as we got regarding their crossing the Atlantic.

And it wasn't all one sided, they wanted to know all about the London and Plymouth blitz.

One day I asked "Why do you call New York, New York City, and Kansas, Kansas City, and so on. We call Truro, Truro, and Plymouth, Plymouth, and yet they are cities. Over the weeks ahead this became a bond between us, Hank would remind us "Call it Truro City from now on John, every time you call it that, think of us." I often do, especially when visiting Truro City.

Jean relates a story that I had long since forgotten, when the GIs placed a basin over our heads (the boys I hope, not the girls) and cut our hair. Thank goodness there were no cameras then, however Jean insists that one of the Yanks took a photo of the camp's barber shop.

One rainy day, Mum suggested that we make 'the boys' a pasty each, and so pasties were made. Note that I have not called them Cornish pasties. I sawed and chopped the wood to stoke the fire, while Anne and Jean cut up the home-grown potatoes, swede, and onions and Mum made the pastry. Now she was a good cook, the best; however, as I have said, pastry was not her speciality. Neighbours must have thought we had chosen a new Pope; the range had its throttle wide open, the kitchen windows steamed over.

At length the pastry was rolled out, turned over and rolled again by Mum; the ash on her cigarette was getting longer, flour sprinkled on the wooden table. Finally the pastry was cut round with a saucepan lid; never had we carried out the task in hand with so much enthusiasm.

The pasties were delivered to the GIs on trays covered in cloths and we left our friends sitting on wooden stools, at a wooden table; we were off, scarpering as fast as we could. Later there was a knock at the door, and Mo, the youngest of the team was standing there. "Gee Mam," he drawled, "that was real swell." Then handing Mum the empty shell of what was once a pasty, he continued, "Would you mind filling it up again."

Mum was never allowed to forget those words.

Mary and June had befriended some American sailors, who were crew members from an LST moored at King Harry. Often in the evenings, during April there would be a gathering on the shore under our house. The sailors, about five or six of them, would arrive in a landing craft, and my sisters, would sit on the rocks with them and flirt.

They were all young, I doubt if there one of them over twenty years of age. The girls in their best frocks, the sailors dressed in bell bottom trousers and white pork-pie hats on the back of their heads.

When the girls were asked "Why are you wearing all white?" they answered, "it's Whitsun, everyone wears white at Whitsun."

As one, the sailors took of their white hats and threw them on the rocks. As I said, youngsters enjoying themselves as youngsters do and I still picture the scene, with joy and sadness, mostly sadness.

There was one sailor, Johnny who never went ashore with his shipmates; he was with his true love – his landing craft – on the water just off shore. Often he would edge into the shore, pick us up and then back out away from the rocks. We would sit on board, and chat, the engine blowing bubbles out of the exhaust as it ticked over.

Johnny talked of many things, most of which I have forgotten, but one I haven't. "I wish I could swim like you".

Once or twice we were taken for a short trip in his landing craft, taking it in turns to steer.

Bob and I were in bed, just talking; the light bulb had been removed because we had recently been visited by the river patrol, who said that a light was showing from our bedroom. This was a time when the invasion fleet was growing in numbers, and everyone was security conscious, or ought to have been, and so reading in bed was out. There

was one advantage to this, with the blackout curtains removed we could see out, often seeing the searchlights at Falmouth scanning the skies.

Anne and Jean were singing, the doors were open, their harmonies drifting along the landing. Then above the singing we heard it, the sirens were sounding, a distant sound of an aircraft could be heard. Looking out of the window told us, this is what we had been waiting for; the Junkers 88 was over St Mawes heading north. Slippers on, out of the front door, up the drive, the girls in their dressing gowns, bob in his pyjamas, me in pyjama bottoms only. Up the drive we ran racing a German bomber – we had to win, we had to see how they liked it, being on the receiving end.

Looking over our shoulders we could just make out the silhouette of the bomber as it banked for the return low-level part of its sortie; we would be just in time. Our parents and older sisters would be looking out of the kitchen window, unaware that we were in on the action; they would be waving and the pilot might be returning their gesture, but he was about to receive the American version, an anti-aircraft shell.

Silence, not a sound, the guns stood motionless. The sergeant had seen the danger and ordered "hold fire". The German had flown between the gun and the row of LSTs. Hit the plane they might have, but firing a shell into the ships was a real possibility lying just half a mile away, three abreast, loaded with tanks, and petrol.

We could imagine the German pilot laughing. The Junkers whistled pass, I could have hit it with my catapult, guns opened up from ships, and from shore batteries, mostly very wide of the target. The noise all around was horrendous; the GIs had been face to face with the enemy for the first time. We stood on the wall, would the German dare make another?

"Pass," I shouted at the top of my voice.

"It will make another attempt," a deep American voice shouted, "get your head down boy that's a German plane." The bomber was lost from view; the sky over the mouth of the Estuary was alight with tracer fire.

Every ship in the harbour together with the battery at St Mawes had opened up. Gradually the gunfire stopped. The aircraft didn't return that night or ever again, rumours had it that it had been shot down. We went home to our beds; a part of me hoped that our visitor had escaped. He

In this sketch the American gun site can be seen between the cottages. The Junkers 88 , passing over out house, is between the gun and the moored LSTs.

had never once, on his many missions, shown any aggression, but I know he was not there just for the fun of it.

Jo came from New York City, he was of Italian origin, dark hair and brown eyes. Together with Mo (of the returned pasty fame and the youngster of the gun crew), we would spend hours fishing aboard the *Swordfish*. They loved it, and sweat would run down their faces. It was thirsty work and the Pandora Inn was always a welcome sight, "Two glasses of your best, barman, and a couple of lemonades for the crew."

One day Mo was off duty, "Can we go out in the boat," he asked. Ambrose Littleton and I were about to do just that, going nowhere special, just 'messing about on the water'. We eased the boat slowly towards him. Mo, standing on the shore leaned forward to pull her in. Grabbing hold of the gunnels, he overstretched, often done by experienced boatmen (and many more times by the inexperienced ones), his hands gripping the boat, his toes digging into the rocks. He could not help himself, pushing the boat away from the shore he was stretched out horizontally.

There was only one outcome to the predicament he was in, he had no choice. When his strength had gone, he just laughed then let go and under he went, then surfacing still wearing his woolly hat!

His cloths were put through the mangle and hung out to dry. Dad's wardrobe was raided and

Mo was dressed in oversized rolled up trousers, held up with braces, and a white shirt with no collar.

At last we set off, rowing a little, drifting a lot, just the three of us, teenagers, chatting about what we would do when we grew up. Dreams of the future were shared. Mo made us promise that we would one day visit him back home, and he rambled on about what we would do, places he will take us. I saw him in a different light – out of uniform – laughing, his youth more apparent away from solders, dressed as soldiers. He looked just a high school boy.

We had stopped rowing; it was a fine spring day in May 1944, Mo was stretched out across the centre seat just his head visible. Ambrose was lying down in the bows, a barrage balloon sail as his mattress, his hands resting on the gunnels. I was in my favourite position, lying on the ribs in the bilges looking up at the sky, legs against the gunnels and feet sticking up into the air. Our retired sea captain friend looking through his 'glass' would have smiled, just a pair of hands in the bow, a head amidships, and a pair of feet near the stern. But he would not have known, and neither did I at the time, aboard the boat were three teenagers, for one of whom the dangers of war were all but over, while for the other two the serious business was about to begin.

In the following weeks and months I became convinced that Mo sensed those moments of peace, as we drifted with the tide, because without saying a word he took off his 'dog tags' (identity disks) from around his neck and placed them next to a waterlogged packet of Camel cigarettes. For just a little while he was free, a civilian.

There was shouting from the shore, it was Innis and Gwen Dorrian-Smith, middle-aged sisters from Greatwood House, Mylor, whom we had often helped with their seine net. They called us "the scallywags".

On this particular day the net contained mullet and flat fish. A week or so later Miss Innis and Miss Gwen were on the beach, catching shrimps. They shouted to us, "Thank your chums for their help with the net".

I told them that Ambrose had started his officer training in the army, and Mo was an American GI,

US army personnel crowd aboard an LST. Their 'flamboyance and laughter' would soon give way to a more sombre mood as D Day approached.

who, in all probability was fighting in France. They just said, "Pull the other one!"

We hadn't seen the sailors and their landing craft for some time, and so when we saw them heading our way, all the gang were waiting. However the mood on the shore that night was more subdued than on their previous visits; the flamboyance and laughter from the US sailors had gone, and now there were only four of them. Mary and June sat side by side with their 'special' friends; there were long spells of silence. Johnny was alone offshore in his landing craft, another Johnny, Johnny Johnson, came over to where I was sitting.

"John, somebody, has to know," he said. "We have been through hell." After a pause he continued (and I clearly remember his every word), "Ships were sinking, men in the water on fire, screaming. There was nothing we could do to help."

I have never forgiven myself for not taking his words more seriously, and listened more intently to what he so desperately wanted to say. I know now that I should have given him a friendly ear. However to me the facts just didn't fit, the invasion fleet was there moored offshore, the wireless had made no mention regarding the start of the invasion. "It must have been a torpedo," I said.

"No, there was gunfire, lots of it, High speed ships, and there was nothing we could do to help those guys."

Author's sketch of LST 289 being towed up the Fal after being damaged during Operation Tiger.

Although I never forgot the conversation on the shore that evening, and the doubts I had, it would be many years before the true story of Exercise Tiger, with the loss of hundreds of lives off the shores of Devon and Dorset, would be made public. Then and only then did I realise that I had turned a deaf ear when an eye witness so wanted to 'pass on' details of that major tragedy.

Days later a badly damaged LST passed close to us as we were fishing. Tugs were towing it up to the King Harry reaches. It looked as if it had been dropped onto its stern from a great height.

A builder's plaque, probably from an LST. The Photograph inset is of the US LST 289 which was badly damaged by enemy action while taking part in Exercise Tiger.

As I have written earlier, living in a house near the Point was a carpenter and his sister, Mr and Miss Harnett. He was a good tradesman and we would spend many happy hours with him in his workshop, building or restoring items of furniture. However his main expertise was in the building trade, gates, stairways, or doors, you name it he could make it.

This slim-built tall man with a quiet nature walked everywhere, taking large strides when pushing his cart full of his tools. We once asked him why his footsteps were almost twice the length of ours, "If you took longer strides," he joked, "your shoes would last longer." And so we walked, or tried to, beside him, striding our legs out as far as they would go.

Everyone's friend, Mr Harnett, had one big problem, a shortage of hardwood. We did our best bringing back from our many beachcombing trips, odd planks and so on. It helped; nothing was wasted. However it was nowhere near the quantity or quality required.

A meeting was held up 'our tree'; a situation had arisen that would ease Mr Harnett's problems. As I have mentioned, the construction was taking place near Malpas of large pontoons called 'Rhinos'. We had no idea at that time what they were to be used for, but we now know they carried tanks and heavy equipment ashore on D Day before the Mulberry Harbour was in place. Later they were moored in line off the coast of Normandy and used as a breakwater.

After launching at Malpas the pontoons were grounded in creeks up and down the Fal. Two were on the shore under Harcourt, one of which had large heavy planks of teak or mahogany strewn over the deck.

In our defence they were not lashed together, and would have washed overboard long before reaching France. However the following is a confession.

Due to the geographical location of the gun site, the GIs were somewhat cut off where evening entertainment was concerned. The ferry across to the Pandora Inn stopped at five or thereabouts, and the last bus to Truro was early evening. For those wishing to attend the dances held at Mylor Bridge or Falmouth, a boat trip to Mylor Harbour was the only option and the *Swordfish* was favourite. A mile or so by boat would save eight or ten miles walking – each way. When we were approached we explained that lending the boat was out of the question, owners of every vessel were responsible for immobilising their craft after dark.

So, on the one hand we needed help 'salvaging' large planks of timber, on the other the GIs longed to have the 'last dance' with English girls. So a deal was agreed and Mr Harnett – unknown to him at the time – would be back in business. We would undertake the ferrying side of things.

It was not, for us, that straightforward. To be caught on the water at night, only a week or so from the invasion date, could have been, at best, the end of the *Swordfish*. But the Yanks had nothing to lose, they could hardly have been put in clink just before the 'big day', and they knew it.

And so 'Operation Timber' was put into action. The conditions were ideal, high tide, and a reasonably calm sea. Bob and Terry were not too keen, so Ted, Hank and Jo, plus myself and one other set off in the late evening dusk. We had plenty of rope and were well briefed; silence was mandatory, just the creaking and splashing of the oars.

Throwing a line over a bollard on the pontoon three of us were on board in no time. We placed two planks at the side of the pontoon on to which we stacked large, heavy planks each one taking two of us to lift. Lashing them together and using other planks as levers, over the side they went with a splash that could have been heard as far away as the Pandora Inn.

Ted was taking care of the boat ready to take us off and the operation lasted no more than ten minutes. We were soon on our way back, towing a raft of the very best timber. Thank goodness the tide was in our favour.

We rounded the point with the raft in tow, and landed just under a clump of young conifers. Casting off, the raft carried on to the shore where eight or ten 'navvies' in GI's uniforms carried them, two to each plank, and quietly stacked them out of sight. Within 20 minutes the operation was over. It had been agreed that Mr Harnett would not be told anything about the operation until after the invasion had taken place.

In the surrounding area today, sixty-five years later, there are houses with bannisters roofs and doors made by a craftsman from the very best timber. To those people lucky enough to live there, and perhaps wonder where the wood came from – I know, 'from under a mulberry bush!'.

Today there are living at Restronguet Point a dedicated team known as 'Friends of Restronguet Point'. I quote from a report of January 2009 from Commander Jonathan Rich and his wife Marianne, the present owners of one of the properties. "I am not aware of what work was carried out by our predecessors who would have re-roofed before us. However, we did find at least one joist that was of extremely heavy construction and definitely looked 1940s era."

Chapter 9

HEAVEN

Dad came up trumps, after all he was in the River Patrol, and if by chance we were caught it would not have gone down too well, his son out on the water after dark. I have always had a sneaking suspicion that he had spoken to the estuary patrol crew.

Percy the pig was getting fatter by the day thanks to the swill from the gun site and so Dad was happy to take the GIs over in the *Steep Holmer* during daylight hours, and didn't impose any restrictions on us regarding the return journey in the early hours of the morning.

Dad was not aware of 'Operation Timber' and over the following week I made three trips to Mylor Harbour, the first being the most memorable. I was alone, the sea was flat calm, the moon had set. I left home about 11.30pm. Having first given the net a once over, I crossed the mouth of Restronguet Creek then hugged the shore under Greatwood House where the sea touched the trees at high tide, and because the salt stopped any growth there was a straight line, just as if a giant had used a trimmer, leaving an upside down hedge. If I heard the Patrol Boat I could have slipped under the canopy into darkness, disappearing from sight. But I didn't see, or hear it.

It was a peaceful time to be on the water. After a sunny day phosphorescent light could be seen where the oars disturbed the surface, leaving a trail of light behind the boat, and as the oars moved through the water they created small whirlpools of light, which on the way back fascinated the

A modern aerial photograph taken looking down on to Restronguet Point. No doubt a number of the houses shown benefited from the author's childhood escapade in 'liberating' the timber.

Americans, many of whom were out in a small boat at night for the first time.

Never had I seen the water so calm or so quite. The tannoys on the LSTs had stopped; the waiting ships were in total darkness, just silhouettes, not a single light was to be seen. The world had gone to sleep.

I still consider myself privileged to have been chosen in some way to experience a sight that can never be repeated, the memories I have were made possible by war with its blackout restrictions. Looking up into the heavens, stars, planets, and the Milky Way shone with clarity far beyond my writing talent to relate, there being no light pollution, and very little air pollution.

The sky was in 3D, the nearest stars stood out in many different colours. I could see the largest twice, one shining above, the other reflected in the sea. Right down to the far horizon stars shone.

I let the *Swordfish* slow down until she was stationary in the water, then I stood on the stern seat to get a full view, looking down into the clear water where the stars' reflections were suspended below the surface. I was in space, from north to south, the Milky Way arching overhead, encircling the earth. I could quite clearly see the countless millions of small stars that made up the outer edge of our galaxy. For the only time that I can remember, stars produced shadows.

Over the many years since that night, I have used those very same heavenly bodies to navigate the oceans, always remembering a night, when as a boy I looked up from a small boat and gazed at the universe. Fish swam by, leaving a sparkling trail, looking like comets or shooting stars. That night, within sight of ships loaded with weapons of war, as nation fought nation, peace prevailed and our planet was at one with the Universe.

Of all the sights I witnessed during my childhood – and there were many – none surpassed the night I drifted through space in a small boat.

I have often wondered if perhaps an American serviceman on board one of the landing craft moored nearby was unable to sleep due to thoughts of what the future might hold for him, and stood at the ship's rail and looked up at the vastness of it all, and thought of home. While at the same time his folks back home, in the United States of America stood on their porch looking up at those same stars, and thought of him.

It is a sad fact that many children living near large cities today have been cut off from the light of stars and the rhythms of night and day.

I was brought back to earth by a whistle; flicking my lighter in acknowledgement I went in alongside the quay. There was a problem; two of the GIs were scared to pass Mylor Church in the dark and they were on the beach further up the creek. We picked them up and there was a lot of leg pulling, but I have to confess, at that time churchyards gave me goose pimples too.

Looking back to that night and our two 'Buddies' who were nervous of passing a church where bodies lay at rest, and yet in a little while, in daylight and darkness, those same young men would undoubtedly pass sights that do not bear thinking about. In war we grew up faster than our year's record.

We later made two more trips to Mylor Harbour; Dad in his motor boat during daylight, while Ted came with me on another trip. We only once heard the patrol boat; it was a long way off.

Chapter 10

GOODBYE AND GOOD LUCK

The date of the forthcoming invasion was a closely-guarded secret known only to the top brass. However everyone knew that it must be imminent. In Truro and the surrounding areas the number of American servicemen had diminished sharply as they were confined to camp. Lorries that had carried men in denim dress, were now full of men in fighting gear, and were heading towards disembarkation points. Ships in the Fal estuary increased in numbers.

From our house we could clearly see LSTs loading troops at Turnaware Point. An exclusion zone of 100 yards had been set up around vessels moored in the area.

It was June's Birthday on the 2 June, and a party had been arranged for the following day, a Saturday. Everyone was dressed in party attire, my sisters and Violet had on their summer dresses, boys wore white shirts and a tie, faces washed, hair brushed.

But there was obviously something 'going on', both Mary and June were on tenterhooks, continually looking out of the window.

Then a shout of excitement, "They're coming!" We looked out and heading towards us at high speed was a landing craft. The wind was fresh, she was continually disappearing in a cloud of spray.

Up the garden they came, four US sailors, proudly carrying a three-tier iced cake, a work of art. Each tier had a hole in the centre, each layer looking like large doughnut. Then everyone was singing 'Happy birthday to you', but there were no candles – perhaps just as well.

The store cupboard had been raided, food that had been 'put aside for a rainy day had been brought out; this was more than a birthday party and everyone knew it, and the reasons behind such lavish preparations. Looking at the table with its fare it would have been hard to believe that there was rationing and shortages.

Equipment being loaded onto 'Rhinos' – barges that had been assembled at Malpas to be towed across the Channel for the D Day invasion.

Johnny was taking care of his craft; he had given orders to "bring my tea down". The sponge cake was cut into slices and handed around on plates, it looked so good. I took a large bite, ran out into the garden and spat it out, where others joined me. In order to protect their work of art from the spray, the sailors had stowed it in the engine compartment. Whether the petrol taste was from the fumes or a leaking pipe I cannot say, however one thing I will say, it was not edible.

There was disappointment and embarrassment all round after all, a lot of effort had been put in for this very special day. June understandably burst into tears, Mum became flustered, and there was only one thing we could do in a situation like this, scarper! And naturally we made for the beach.

Shouting to Johnny to pick us up we climbed aboard the landing craft. How many of us went I cannot say, however my brother, and two sisters, plus Violet, Ted, and Terry, Johnny Johnson and one of his buddies. Then we were off with the wind behind us, heading for the line of LSTs moored two or three abreast. The following sea, colliding with our wash, caused the spray to leap into the air. Never had we covered so much sea in so short a time. This was to be one of the most memorable days of our childhood. Seven children in party attire had a unique opportunity to say 'Goodbye and Good luck'.

Standing on a wooden rail on the side, holding on with one hand waving with the other, we motored down the line of ships. Men in battle gear started to move towards the rails and waved back. Johnny was standing at the wheel and at the end of the line we turned to starboard and continued down the coast of St Just in Roseland, until turning near the sunken freighter we started the return run.

The number of men at the rails had increased; the throttle was wide open, the sea was giving us a rough ride, we held on tight to stop ourselves being thrown about as the flat-bottomed craft pounded the waves. Party dresses and white shirts were getting wet, hair brushed with love and pride by Mum hung limp, dampened by salt spray, but we didn't care.

We turned into the wind to make the return pass, the spray came over, dampness turned into a drenching, we were laughing and the girls were screaming at the same time. Johnny and his shipmates had taken their hats off and were enjoying every minute. We were only fifty feet away from the invasion fleet. Regulations had been thrown to the wind.

About one week later we had a visit. A landing craft pulled in under our house. On board was a US naval officer and two other sailors we recognised. The passed us and went up to the house where they briefly spoke to Mum before returning. Johnny Johnson, June's friend – Johnny the skipper of the landing craft, and another of those who had taken us on that trip, had all drowned off Omaha beach.

Chapter 11

FROM FALMOUTH WITH ORDERS

I was out of bed early on 5 June 1944. We had word that roads were closed to traffic, and there would be no buses. Mary, June and I were preparing to set off early to walk the five miles to Truro City.

I sat at the kitchen window eating breakfast, looking out over the Carrick Roads, and beyond, over the English Channel. There were ships everywhere, from the coast to the horizon the gathering armada was moving, from tugs to liners, destroyers to landing craft. Oh for a camera!

Barrage balloons tugged on their cables in the strong wind, like mackerel on a fishing hook. Naval craft were dashing in all directions giving orders by flashing their Aldis lamps at high speed. The LSTs were being manoeuvred into the channel by a variety of harbour craft, blue exhaust smoke showing their power and urgency of the task in hand.

Why I didn't stay home from school and watch I really don't know, after all there were no buses and school was over five miles away.

Ships were leaving for the greatest invasion in history, right before our eyes.

The three of us set out walking at a fast pace. At the top of the hill opposite the farm I stopped and had one last look. We had, over the past months, seen many LSTs sailing up and down the channel. However, this time they were showing what they were capable of, for the very first time they had a bow wave, and there was a sense of urgency and purpose. Reluctantly I dragged myself away. I knew then that I was witnessing history, and that the memory would remain with me forever. I am certain that, along the coast there would be men and boys watching who shared my thoughts, felt the adrenalin in their bodies, and wished they were going with them.

Torn between history lessons at school, or history in the making, I joined the girls who were ahead of me. On we walked, mile after mile, not a single motor car passed us, and not a single human being either. From Playing Place we carried on down the long, winding main Truro to Falmouth road. Today thousands of motorists pass along that road, on 5 June 1944 just three of us had it to ourselves; we walked alone down the centre of the road. As we levelled off at the

This sketch, from memory, shows all the seaborne activity in the confined area from St Antony light to Penarrow Point at 0645 double British summer time 5 June 1944 – the view from 'Steep Holm'.

This is the window that Mr Rowe looked out that morning. Probably it has been replaced over the years.

bottom of the hill we heard the sound of an engine approaching. It was a small green coloured Post Office telephone maintenance van. When it stopped my sisters got into the front with the driver while I climbed into the back and crouched on the floor, surrounded by tools, coils of wire and other paraphernalia.

Under the railway bridge, on up the hill the little Morris van struggled down through the gears. Had it been the blackberry season Mary could have opened the window and picked a few!

I arrived at school 15 minutes late. Mr Rowe, who had taken over as Headmaster, was standing on the stairs staring out of the large window at the sky, deep in thought.

"Good morning John. You are late, no buses?"

"No Sir, I walked most of the way."

"Well done," he looked down, we were alone on the stairway, putting his hand at the side of his mouth he quietly asked "Any sign of activity, any movement"?

One would have thought that a German agent was hiding in a nearby cupboard. "Yes Sir, I watched the ships leave."

He put his hand on my shoulder, a look of emotion showed on his face, "Thank you, go to all the classes and ask that everyone assemble in the hall." I left him there still looking up at the sky.

After prayers, and singing a favourite hymn, 'For Those in Peril on the Sea', the head addressed us. These are his exact words "Every one of us in future years will remember this day. God be with them all."

The buses were running again later that afternoon and at four-thirty I was on my way home. Arriving at Harcourt I stood by the gate from where I had seen the ships leave. My heart missed a beat there they were, anchored in Falmouth Bay, and in the estuary, ships, lots of them, this morning they had left; now they were back. The sky overhead was full of barrage balloons.

After tea Bob and I took the hand line and rowed out where we knew we could catch a Pollack or two. It was an excuse; we just wanted to have a closer look at the ships, and although we didn't venture too close, it was near enough to leave me with haunting thoughts for some time afterwards.

We were about a quarter of a mile away from the line of moored landing craft, and over the background noise of the ships' engines (they had been left running) we heard a voice, someone was shouting, loudly.

I scanned the line of ships for anyone standing at the rails, or at least in a prominent position. We were as near as I wanted to go. The person seemed to be desperately trying to attract attention, repeating over and over, "Ahoy! Ahoy there!"

I stood up and scanned the water, nothing, nobody. Keeping our distance we rowed along the line of ships. The shouting continued but there was nothing we could do; I had convinced myself that there wasn't anyone in the water, and so we rowed home, although the shouting continued getting further away as we did so.

There is no ending to this story, who he was, what did he want? A message to pass perhaps, or a letter to post? Help of some kind was needed, but none could be given. Not by us.

Chapter 12

D DAY

The following morning 6 June 1944, the ships were gone; once again the roads were closed. For the second day in succession my sisters and I walked to Truro, and were on time.

The radio had given news of the invasion; there was excitement in the air. As we walked down over Lemon Street a lady opened her front door, and walked through an opening where once an iron gate had been, before being taken, along with railings, for 'the war effort'. She held her clasped hands as if in prayer, looking across towards the Cathedral, quite oblivious to our close presence. Emotionally she pleaded, "Please, my boy."

It might have been a holiday as far as normal lessons were concerned. Mr Rowe brought in radio sets he had made, valves on boards would be the best way to describe them today. He tried to get signals direct from the beaches with little success, only lots of whistling and Morse code. However news updates were frequently given, and our troops' positions marked on maps. Truro Senior Boys School looked like a control room that day.

Midday we had a treat, a building opposite the school gates had been taken over as a doughnut factory for the GIs. Due perhaps to security, production had continued overnight and ladies brought out traysful. Doughnuts were new to this country then; never have they tasted as good as the first ones did, on D Day.

On arriving home we discovered that our American friends at the gun site had left, the site was deserted and a ghostly atmosphere hung over the area, made worse perhaps by not knowing where they had gone, or not having been given the chance to say goodbye.

Ships, equipment, and fighting men go ashore on Omaha Beach, Normandy.

After tea we sat on the wall where the guns had been and reminisced. Terry recalled the time his Mum had bought a mangle and Hank had volunteered to collect it with a lightweight collapsible hand cart – the type used by airborne troops. He started down the hill from Harcourt, first walking then running faster and faster as the cart with its heavy load took over. Just over half way down it became obvious that the cart was in control and pulling the American and there was nothing for it but to let go. Over went the cart, mangle and all. The cast iron frame smashed, it had wrung its last wring.

Hank vowed to find a replacement and we went with him and waited outside each house; sometimes he was gone quite a while, other times he was back in no time, and who can wonder at it. Opening the door to a six-foot-two-inch Yank, with a chat up line to beat all others, "Excuse me Mam, I'm looking for a man-gal."

One can only wonder at the responses he got, but credit where credit's due he came up trumps, and we helped him push the replacement up hills, and hold it back going down. Fifteen years after the war I called on Mrs Blackburn at her house in Devoran, and there standing near the back door was the mangle.

Sitting on the wall, we recalled the days, usually a Saturday, when the GIs had a bath at our house, a luxury for them, especially as Saturday night was dance night. The joy they must have felt just to have a soak in a hot bath is understandable. Having crossed the Atlantic in a crowded ship where sea sickness must have added to their discomfort, housed on arrival at Southampton in 'make do' accommodation, then living in tents with only basic washing facilities and limited water supplies. Water had to be brought in by bowser there being no mains water supplies at Restronguet at that time.

Preparation for their bath day was a team effort, those in the queue sawed and chopped logs from railway sleepers. The Cornish range would glow hot, heating the water. Stoking the fire was our job. The sleepers had been coated with tar and so black smoke belched from the chimney.

We had two bathrooms so it was a conveyer belt operation. The girls would make coffee to which Margaret's tinned milk ration was added, served together with sugar and cookies provided by courtesy of the US Government. Mum provided clean towels that had been boiled in an electric boiler, a luxury then as most households had a copper house where the washing was done in a boiler fuelled with household waste. The towels had been scrubbed with Imp soap – 3d for 3 tablets – then dried in the sea air on a line held up with a yacht's spar found on the beach.

And so the reminiscing continued; we were going to miss the Yanks, and we were not the only ones. Percy the pig had lived on the very best swill, he was growing bigger and fatter by the day. He would now have to scoff boiled potatoes, sour apples, and acorns, there being very little in the way of 'scraps' in our household.

It was Saturday 10 June 1944, Bob and I were busy in the vegetable garden when we heard a shout, it was Jack the ferryman.

Jack was a good friend of ours, we often stood in for him ferrying passengers across to the Pandora side when he was otherwise engaged. In return he turned a blind eye if we did the odd trip at a time when there was no official service.

Jack sounded excited as he shouted to us, "Quick the Yanks are in a field over at Mylor, and they want to see you, you will have to hurry they are leaving this morning".

Ted and Terry were nowhere to be seen so Bob and I jumped aboard the ferry. I took one oar, Jack the other, rowing and giving directions at the same time. It must have been the fastest crossing ever made. Jumping on to the shore, we started to run and by the time we had gone one hundred yards up the hill, two locals shouted to us, "The Yanks want to see you." It seemed that the whole neighbourhood had been asked to get in touch with us.

As per directions we took the first right, at the top of the hill, on past the copse where British troops manning an anti-aircraft gun were based. Here we were stopped by US Military Police, smartly dressed and wearing white steel helmets inscribed with 'MP'.

They stood in the centre of the road blocking our way into the field, or so we thought. The sergeant looked down at us smiling he knew what we were thinking, "Are you Ted or John?" he asked. That is the absolute truth, in the two fields were hundreds of American troops, waiting to be shipped to France, and yet the Military Police Sergeant overseeing security, knew our names.

"They are expecting you, but how the hell you are going to find them is your problem. I'll come in with you." He escorted us to the centre of the first field. Every square foot was packed with GIs, some sitting in groups, other's lying down, eyes closed. All were dressed in combat gear, a steady procession was moving towards the adjoining field where lorries were waiting. Packed kit bags were left at the gate and were being loaded into nearby trucks; time was running out, were we too late, had we missed them?

Our new friend the MP left us in the middle of the field, with instructions, "The field through the gate is out of bounds, half an hour only, stay here they will see you." he said

And they did. We didn't see them, or hear their shouts, we didn't need to. At least eight GIs sitting on the grass near to where we were standing drew our attention to a group over near the hedge who were waving, they had spotted us.

Over the comparatively short time we had known them, a mutual bond had developed between us; it was impossible to judge who were the most excited at our reunion, added to which we all knew that in all probabilities we would not

see each other again. That day was in many ways was unique, two children ten and fourteen years old, who had been 'blooded by war', here we were, meeting with young men from a foreign country, who would have to pass through that barrier in a very short time from now.

"They've put us into the infantry," the sergeant said. "We've had no training. Yesterday we were in the 477 Battery Battalion, today the infantry! We are foot soldiers, and scared!" His troop looked on nodding approvingly while he continued, "We get very little news, how are things going over there?"

Dwight Eisenhower was comparatively unknown to the British people at that time. However we had a lot of faith in Montgomery, or Monty as he was affectionately known. He had after all given England and her allies their first major land victory, driving Rommel back across the North African desert, and had established a reputation as a top class leader.

One of my 'jobs' at home was cutting up newspapers into squares, tying a piece of string in one corner and hanging them in the lavatory, this gave me plenty of time to keep abreast of the news – getting two opportunities to get an update into the current situation. Yes, in June 1944, I relayed the news so desperately sought that I had acquired sitting on the lavatory that morning reading from squares of newspaper. This I imparted to the American infantry who were about to enter battle. "The voice of a schoolboy".

The words I then spoke I truly believed in at that time. "The worst bit is over," I said. "The troops are ashore and moving inland, once a foothold has been established, tanks and equipment will be brought ashore in large numbers, and a breakthrough will be made." I was relaying it word by word as reported in the *Daily Sketch*, no more, no less.

With hindsight I became more than a little over-confident, "By the time you get there the worst part will be over. I wish I was coming with you. You will be home for Christmas."

How wrong I was. Heavy fighting continued no further away from us than say Portland was. At night time with the wind in the south-easterly direction, we often heard the sound of distant explosions, it was then, most of all that we thought of our friends, and wondered.

It was time to say goodbye, we were given items they didn't or couldn't take with them, such as 'candy'. By far the most memorable item was two pairs of large red leather boxing gloves.

We walked to the departure gate with our friends, the sergeant looked straight head, head up. "John," he said in a voice loud enough for me to hear, yet not for the ears of those making their way to the trucks, "We had strict orders to spike all canned food and bury it before leaving, you know I can't remember spiking those cans. Five paces from the edge of the gorse and five paces from the path, you will see a stone." Each and every one of them shook our hands. Hank looked down as he took my hand, "don't forget, it's Truro 'City' from now on."

I shouted to Mo as he was about make his way into the next field, he had asked me if I would sell him my 'lucky' silver lighter, but after some hesitation I said no. After all, I had held that lighter during the Plymouth Blitz, relit candles that had been blown out by the blast of a bomb, fought for it, been expelled from school because of it, countless fires were started with it on the shores of the River Fal, I had signalled to my friends waiting on Mylor Quay, how could I part with my lucky charm?

I caught him up, "Look Mo," I said "I cannot sell it, it might break its lucky spell, so you can borrow it." Handing it to him I said "Send it back when you get home, Jo has my address."

And so they went to war, a boy too young to shave, and my silver cigarette lighter, which I had swapped for a model of the French liner *Normandy*. It was now going to the area which gave that beautiful ship its name, and which, was now lying on its side in New York harbour.

Restronguet Point became Treasure Island on Monday 12 June. Ted, Terry, Bob and me, were putting on the accent, acting the part, "Five paces from the gorse, me hearties, the same from the path." We had no map, we didn't need one; the flat stone could be seen as soon as we arrived. The first tin was only just under the ground, it was the largest food tin we had ever seen, khaki in colour, with stencilled numbers printed together with its contents.

We shared them out as ordered, tins of peaches, ham, corned beef, and so on. Mum hid our share in the piano 'With an iron frame'.

Chapter 13

REALITY

If we thought things would return to normal now that the invasion fleet had left, how wrong we were. About a week later we arrived home from school and there they were, two hospital ships, one larger than the other, moored about a quarter of a mile offshore. Looking like Mississippi ferry boats without stern paddles, they had tall narrow funnels, a low freeboard and a wide beam. Large white crosses were painted on their hulls.

We couldn't wait; a new adventure was in the offing. We had developed a sixth sense for such things, friends who were present when the 'boat went out' jumped aboard, there was no discrimination between sexes, boys and girls were equals.

Dressed in boating gear – short trousers and bare feet – we set off on a short reconnaissance mission, after all they were in our patch, our territorial waters, we had every right to know, why they were there.

There was no doubt that these vessels were inland steamers in peace time with their low freeboard and shallow draught, and with a large white bridge superstructure. They had no names or means of identification. Regrettably I never saw their engines, wood burning, and steam I bet, how I would like to have met members of their crew

Author's sketch from memory of the hosptial ships in the Fal river.

who must have had one hell of a trip across the Atlantic, what stories they could have told. Why were those ships there, where had they been? We had a theory – they came from the beaches of Normandy. With their shallow draft and low freeboard they were easy accessed from smaller ships transferring wounded for immediate attention.

We slowly passed along the side of the largest vessel, surveying all that we spied. Built like a real ship with riveted plates (most American ships built at that time were welded), rust streaks marked their once white hulls. They had tasted salt water after a life on a river, and it showed. That was her outward appearance; I was not prepared for the sights one of them held, tucked away below decks.

Standing in an open doorway was a middle aged couple. We passed within hailing distance, and rowed toward them. I will for the sake of this book call them Bert and Daisy. They were from London, they said, and had moved to Cornwall to be near their family who lived in Penryn. We didn't go on board then, but Daisy had asked if I could bring out some fresh milk and water, they were 'gasping' for a decent cuppa.

That evening I rowed out alone to the hospital ship taking the promised milk in a screwtop bottle, and water in a biscuit tin. Tying the *Swordfish* up alongside, I climbed aboard. The caretakers had made their quarters in a cabin under the bridge; they ate, slept and lived in this area. It was cosy and warm, outwardly, an ideal retreat, just lying there, letting a troubled world sort out its own problems. Cooking was carried out on a paraffin stove, and lighting was by an oil lamp. The portholes were covered over to stop any light shining out. There was no radio, or of course, newspapers. They were cut off from the outside world.

Over a cup of cocoa we talked, or to be more precise, Daisy talked – she was the boss, and city-wise. "We are told," she said "that these vessels were to be taken out into deep water and sunk; they had served their purpose, and were now surplus to requirements. "There are areas," she continued, "that were out of bounds..." And she pointed her finger at two large watertight doors on the opposite side of the gangway, "...through those."

The next evening Bob and myself, had been spinning for mackerel, we had caught a dozen or so, and armed with four, plus milk and water we pulled alongside, and were soon sitting in the cabin. Bert was very quiet, he and Bob engaged themselves in a game of draughts, Daisy and I walked along a gangway that stretched from one side of the vessel to the other. Leaning on the rail she said that her husband wanted to go home, he couldn't sleep, and could hear noises, sometimes during the day and sometimes at night, a moaning sound that echoed through the ship. Once he heard a high pitched screeching and wailing, but more often it was a continuous moaning, lasting for a minute or so.

To her surprise I laughed, "Let's go and speak to him" I said. We got into the *Swordfish*, Bert and I, and rowed to the bow of the hospital ship. She was moored by large ropes to a buoy, which was about twelve feet long; heavy wooden fenders were attached to the sides, and a large ring was on the top. These buoys were everywhere, the LSTs had been tied up to them before sailing, but they had been moored fore and aft; the two new arrivals were only moored at the bow and they were free to 'swing'.

If it was calm and as the tide turned, the vessel would run down on the buoy, scrapping its side, the sound it made wood-on-wood metal-on-metal made moaning and screeching sound that would have echoed throughout the ship. It was this sound that Bert had heard. I know, I had heard it when rowing home the previous night. Daisy gave me half a crown and asked if I could bring a bottle of stout for Bert, "Bring it tomorrow," she asked. "I wish to speak to you again."

Once again we sat in the cabin, the Londoners, and yours truly. Bert was looking better, he had his bottle of stout, Daisy her cuppa made with well water and fresh milk. She quickly came to the point. "This boat is going to be sunk," she said, " but the store is full of tinned food." My daughter

has a car, we load your boat, after dark, you meet her, half for you half for her, here is a telephone number, ring her and arrange a meeting, how about it?" I was as quick as she was, "Open those doors let me see what's in there, and I will."

There is a part of me that wished I had left well alone. The large iron handles that locked the heavy watertight doors were pulled down, Bert stayed in the cabin while Daisy and I stepped into what was once a large ward.

As we entered this untouched field hospital we were hit by the smell of disinfection, burnt flesh and other things that are better left censored. This vessel and its contents were fresh from the beaches of Normandy. The wide passageway must have been used as an operating theatre, everything was there, untouched, just as it had been in the height of battle, except for the casualties and those attending to their urgent needs.

Many men's lives were saved here, and others were not. Bandages and stained pads were lying everywhere, a pair of broken glasses, battledresses, which had been cut off, were piled high in a corner, a rifle with the wooden butt split in two, as if it had taken the force of a machine gun bullet and possibly used for a splint, who knows. I became aware that I had no shoes on, the steel deck was sticky under my bare feet, this area had run red. Steel helmets were stacked in a corner, one was German.

I'd had enough, running to the side of the ship I felt sick. And even while typing this brings the horror of it back. One can only praise the courage of the medical staff that had carried out their duty in what must have been close proximity to the very heart of battle. Doctors and nurses, must have raised their voices to be heard above the gunfire. And to think that I had wished I could have gone with the invasion fleet on that morning 5 June 1944, as if the whole thing was some kind of a game. The reality, the stark truth was brought home to me that evening. I saw it and smelt it, in its raw state, and I will never forget it.

We have all seen many photographs, dramatic newsreels, and well directed films of battle scenes, however nothing can relay the smell; one has to be there, trying hard not to take deep breaths. Of all our senses, smell triggers memories more vividly than hearing, touch or sight.

There was not a chance that I could carry out my side of the bargain I had made with Daisy alone. There were lots of things I might risk, such as when we took the wood for instance, but this was different. Not only had I never used a telephone, If Dad found out that would be the end of boating.

So I confided in Mum.

Anne and Jean looked after Margaret and the following evening Mum and I rowed out in the dark towards the silhouette of the hospital ships. Mum was wearing a heavy River Patrol overcoat and hat, for the very first time on the water at night I was nervous, and started to shiver and I didn't know why. I missed my lucky cigarette lighter.

It was over in no time, the pow-wow between Daisy and Mum, the loading of tins, shaking of hands. We were on our way home. Two days later we met Daisy's daughter.

I can still see Dad walking down the drive that day, shouting "Have you been on board those hospital ships? The police are searching the area."

We children held a meeting up in 'our tree'. Ideas included burying the items of war at the campsite where just a short while before we had dug up stores left by the GIs, or digging a large hole nearer to home where there would be less of a chance being 'caught in the act'. We set about the digging operation the very next day. At twenty-five paces straight out from our back door, armed with picks and shovels, we dug, and we dug. The task in hand became more of a project than the reasons for doing it. Into the hole went all of our souvenirs, incendiary bombs (live and spent), shrapnel, including the large piece that nearly killed my sisters, Spitfire bits (but not the cockpit canopy, that ended up in a collection), uniforms, steel helmets, 'K' rations, even an American rifle (a relic of the Great War). Everything we had collected went into that hole – well almost everything. There were exceptions, not the tins of food hidden in the piano, or a few hidden in the trees where the salvaged timber had been, or the sack of sugar buried under the coal, or the green candlewick bedspreads with shipping line motives embossed in the centre. Mum kept the latter in her blanket box for the rest of her life.

I had no regrets parting with our souvenirs. PC Steer and his posse never turned up, somehow we knew he wouldn't – not before giving us the wink.

Today if you stand at the back door of the house we had lived in, take between twenty and thirty paces, dig down five feet or so, you will find the rusted mementos of a children's war. However I warn you, they are guarded by a very big yew tree, the healthiest one you will ever see. It started its long life on what was once a vegetable patch, in soil fed with basic slag, fish innards, and pig manure!

Later we watched as tugs towed the Hospital ships away, their destination not known.

It was an order by the Ministry of Food that privately reared pigs had to be handed over at time of slaughter, the owner being paid the same as farmers, and were given the option of retaining up to half the carcass. There were no refrigerators then; Dad did toy with the idea of salting our half down, but nothing came of that. So he settled for a large joint.

Percy had become 'one of us'. He had a very good life – we let him out of his sty when we were able to 'keep an eye' on his wanderings. Sunbathing was his favourite pastime, stretched out on the grass, with a grin on his face. However we often had fun at his expense and Bob and Terry would ride on his back, until one day he rolled over and trapped Bob's leg under his fat self. Percy just lay there, grinning, while we did our best to free Bob, who was not in any pain, he simply couldn't get his leg out.

Bribery, twisting his tail, all were to no avail. There was the squealing: pig not squealing, just grunting, and Bob squealing and laughing at the same time. Then we found a sack and put it over Percy's head and he was up in no time, but the sack stayed firmly in place, and we made no attempt to get it off until the poor pig came to within feet of falling over the bank and on to the shore.

Two men arrived with a small lorry, that had a ramp at the back. They didn't need the sticks they were carrying, we saw to that, and surrounded by his friends patting his back, Percy followed Anne and I up the ramp. In less than five minutes it was all over, Percy was gone.

A plan was drawn up: June gave her full support, Mary who had been given permission to be home late didn't want to 'rock the boat' abstained, but vowed silence. There had to be one hundred per cent support in order to succeed.

All mothers' have a sixth sense when 'something is in the air' and Mum was no exception. That evening, she put every effort into preparing a meal on a par with Christmas. The kitchen was a hive of activity, condensation from saucepans boiling on the stove filled the room, the smell of cooking filled our nostrils, and wetted our appetites. Each taking our place at the table, we watched as the oven door opened; not a word was spoken, thick crackling that had been covered with honey 'sizzled', potatoes, fresh carrots and all the trimmings were placed on the table.

Mum started to dish up, "No pork for us, thank you," I said, "we are not going to eat Percy."

Dad looked surprised, and perhaps a little angry, "And who might I ask is 'we'?" Every one of us raised our hands. Dad must have felt like Captain Bligh did when faced with the mutineers. Up until then Dad's word was law; his authority had never been questioned.

"No pork, no dinner." Apart from our parents, and Mary, eating their meal there was total silence. Homemade rice pudding followed, none for us. After we had helped with the washing up, we went out, down to the shore.

The next morning there was no breakfast, midday no lunch; "Let them build up an appetite," were Dad's last words before going to work. Cold pork, homemade pickled onions, bubble and squeak were placed before us at tea time, not one of us gave way, we would not eat Percy, and out we went, down on to the shore.

The next day was a carbon copy of the day before. For three days there was a repetition of day one, no meals, and for three days we went down to the shore, then walked along out of sight, up to the small clump of firs where we had hidden stores taken from the hospital ships.

Mr Hartnell, who was now a happy man having all the timber he needed thanks to the GIs who were now fighting in France, and children who were fighting for their principles, had a large saucepan of boiled potatoes, and another of home grown vegetables at the ready. Joined by our friends we had a picnic hidden in the fir trees. On the menu, tinned ham followed by tinned peaches, courtesy of Bert and Daisy.

I had some sympathy for Dad, he had after all worked hard in his efforts to become as self sufficient as possible, only to overfeed us to such a degree that we could survive for three days of fasting. The irony of the whole episode was that we had refused to eat Percy, yet we had survived on tinned ham.

We enjoyed our little game, and so I suspect did Mum, she never lost the smile on her face. Nothing was said but on the fourth day when we went in for tea, a tin of ham had been taken from the piano. We had just about had enough tinned ham and boiled potatoes and vegetables. "Thought we would have a change today", said Dad, "and there's plenty left for the next two days!"

Chapter 14

RESCUES AND SALVAGE

In the autumn of 1944 blackout restrictions were lifted for the first time in five years. We were able to look out of the windows at night without the fear of showing a light. It was as if we had lived in a box, the outside world, the sunrise, and the full moon reflecting on the water could only be enjoyed by going out into the garden.

I have often wondered how wildlife was affected by the sudden switching off, of lighthouses, and city illuminations. With this in mind I recall a phenomenon when, at the end of the blackout, we were treated to a spectacular display of 'dancing moths'.

The curtains were drawn back, the lights were on (remember there was nothing but a low hedge and a tree between us and the estuary, the nearest land was a mile and a half away, straight out over the water), and during the late evening every square inch of glass on the window was occupied by a moth. Large and small, all colours, those who could not find a spot on the glass hovered a foot or so away awaiting their turn. They were not silent, the sound of wings flapping, could be clearly heard. They were oblivious to our presence. I was fascinated, hypnotized by their antics, those at the bottom of the window pane clawed their way up to the top and there was a continuous rotation. I held my nose against the glass, my eye just an inch away from them, which made not the slightest difference. I became convinced that they were dancing to the music on the radio, moving up and down together in a wave-like motion.

Where had they come from? Attracted to our light, the only one on that side of the Point, they probably flew across the water from the St Just in Roseland side. I don't know how long a moth lives, but was our light the first they had ever seen, and were attracted to it? Today I am told, moths are to be seen only in ones and twos at Restronguet Point.

Bob met me from the bus when I arrived home from school. "Mum is out in the *Swordfish*," he panted, "she has a boat in tow. Anne and Jean are looking after Margaret."

We ran home, and there about half-a-mile out was Mum who was making, to our knowledge, her first attempt at rowing; and to add to her problems she indeed had another boat in tow.

Now Mum had come from a long line of seafarers. Displayed at the end of the jetty at Burnham-on-sea is a bronze plaque commemorating her grandfather Charles Hunt, and his lifeboat crew, who, on a stormy night put to sea twice in a rowing lifeboat, to go to the aid of two sailing ships in difficulty in the Bristol Channel.

Mum had often been out in the boats, but had never attempted using the large oars that required a strong pair of arms and shoulders to just lift them out of the water. Here we had a lady finding out the hard way that there is more to rowing than meets the eye. At each stroke she was standing up with the oars on the backward stroke, lowering them into the water sitting down, and then taking the pulling stroke. Not to sound unkind she was nearer to flying than rowing, and to make things harder she had the other boat in tow.

She needed help and the tide was taking her towards Falmouth and the English Channel beyond. It was September and the sea was warm. Shouting for my play togs and a towel to be taken down to the shore, I peeled off down to my underpants and swam out to the *Steep Holmer*.

Thankfully the restriction regarding the immobility of the engine had been lifted, the fuel tanks were half full, two swings and she was away. Picking up Bob from the shore we were off in no time. That was the easy part.

Mum had in tow a large ship's life raft, and she wasn't making any forward progress. We had to act as a team, each knowing what to do, and when to do it, as I have mentioned before there was no clutch, if we wished to stop, then the engine would have to stop.

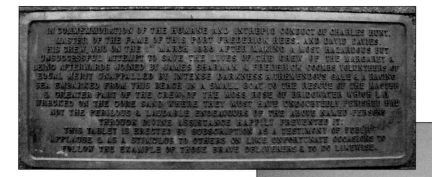

Above: The plaque at Burnham-on-Sea commemorating the bravery of the lifeboat crew.

Right: Charles Hunt, standing in the stern of the Burnham-on-sea Lifeboat. Granddad Hunt is third from the left leaning on the hull with his hand on his hip

This would have to be the first time for Bob, to take over the motor boat (why not he was nearly nine years old after all!) and there was no option, as we came alongside I would jump onboard the *Swordfish*, and take a tow rope.

What a sight we must have looked, in an area where today expensive yachts are moored, in 1944 a small boy in a motor boat towing a rowing boat, which in turn was towing a life raft, added to which there was not enough power to make headway, and I was rowing to help things along, dressed only in my swimming trunks.

We made the raft 'fast' tied to a tree under our house, it had been drifting for some time, the support lines were faded white, and barnacles were growing on the wooden grating.

At tea Mum relayed her afternoon experiences. The raft she said had drifted up the estuary with the tide; she had kept an eye on it until she became convinced that there were men lying down, and that she could see an arm hanging over the side.

By the time that Anne and Jean arrived home from school, Mum had made up her mind to row out and have a look. Considering her limited experience this was a brave decision, and we told her so.

After tea we surveyed our salvage, we soon established that it was upside down, and had been for some time, and through the grating we could see a large square metal container with a screw fitting plug, which was impossible to get at, we pushed the raft back into the water, and I swam under the hull and came up inside looking up through the grating at the others.

One tank was empty and it gave off a hollow sound, the other was full, access to which was via the screw cap, fitted with two flanges. I couldn't move it, even by banging it with a stone, and I wondered if shipwrecked sailors, had the same problem, how frustrating it would have been to know that survival stores were at hand and yet not accessible.

We conjured up theories of the raft's life before it found its way drifting up the River Fal. It was well made, heavily constructed of the finest materials. Its grey paint gave it a naval look, was it from the *Bismarck*, or HMS *Illustrious*? Both had sunk in the Western Approaches. Had it been lying on a beach for some time, an island perhaps?

There was only one way to find out – open the tank. With planks as levers, and rocks to wedge it we inched the raft slowly up until it was balanced upright, then with one final push over it went with a crash.

With a hammer we freed the brass cap. The container was full. Tins of ship's biscuits, tins of milk tablets, tins of chocolate, a knife with a wooden handle, a large rubber-covered waterproof torch, a whistle, first aid kit, and more. We never found any identification marks; even the torch batteries were unmarked. We had great plans for our new craft, anchoring it off shore to store the nets in, a swimming platform, amongst others; we even gave it a name *Mary Celeste*.

Dad had other plans after reporting it to the 'authorities' who had no interest in it. The float, constructed of copper, ended its days in the hands of a scrap merchant who had paid Dad 10 pounds for it, a lot of money then. It kept its origins secret to the end. We had a torch, a whistle and a knife. The chickens had ship's biscuits for tea, and supper.

And so 1944, a momentous year, came to an end. I left school, at fourteen years of age, and for the remaining time we were living in Cornwall. I worked at Solomon and Metz, printers, in Truro City, and although I was happy there it wasn't my cup of tea. I wanted to be involved in radio communications, and that is where I ended up.

We celebrated the end of the war in Europe with a firework display. We had five, one rocket, and four fountains. The ships in Falmouth blew their whistles, and sirens sounded for the last time.

Celebrations were low-key. Teddy Blackburn with whom we had shared so many adventures, contracted rheumatic fever, and was confined to bed. Without him we lost enthusiasm, our childhood spirits had gone, and when the Royal Navy laid up submarines on the sand banks in Devoran Creek we never once had a close look.

There would have been a time when we would have crawled all over them, gone below if possible, had one each. We didn't, Ted was ill, adventure had lost its edge, and added to which we knew that our time in Cornwall was nearing its end.

I finished work on a Saturday at twelve thirty, pay day, and on my way to catch the bus, I heard my name being called, it was an old school friend. "A shop in River Street is selling bananas," he shouted. The last time I had tasted a banana was in 1940, five years previously, and I had pocket money. Off we ran, soon joined by other boys as the news spread.

We joined the queue and patiently waited, would they be rationed? Would I be allowed enough for Mum and Dad and my brother and sisters to have one each, or would we have to have to be content with half, or less?

My turn came, the last wooden box was placed on the counter and opened, the greaseproof paper was peeled back. Well, they smelt like bananas, but they were not the ones that had remained in my memory all those years. They were sun dried, black, small, and not very appetizing.

"How many would you like," asked the lady. "Eight please," I replied a little hesitantly, after all it was the last box and there were quite a few eager customers outside waiting.

I ended up with four black rotten looking something that smelt like bananas, and tasted like one – I think. I ask you to try and describe a banana to someone who has never seen one, then imagine, just for a moment, that you are eleven years old, and the last time you saw one was five years previously. Jean had Margaret's undivided attention, I think.

Chapter 15

THE STEEP HOLMER'S FINALE

Sundays were a day of rest, more especially for Dad who was beginning to feel the strain of five years continuous responsibility, added to which there was the uncertainty of the future; he had bought 'Steep Holm' and knew future employment in the area, with men returning to civilian life, would not be easy.

We were in the sitting room, occupying ourselves with books, games etc. or just looking out of the window at the view and what was going on outside. This 'do-nothing' pastime had taken up a fair amount of our time over the past five years, just looking at, and never being tired of, the view. Very few comings and goings happened 'out there' without our knowledge.

Dad was sleeping in 'his' chair. It was an art deco leather armchair, embedded into which was a large piece of bomb shrapnel. During the blitz it had smashed through the window, and made a large hole in the blackout material, and ended up passing through the back of the chair, where it remained embedded at Mum's request, even after repairs were carried out.

There was a strong wind blowing that day from the west, at the mouth of Restronguet Creek. 'Cats paws', dark patches of water moving fast on the surface, were picking up spray and blowing it along; these are the areas that yacht skippers look for, knowing when to take or be prepared for, a gust to hit them.

Conditions were not ideal for a small sailing craft, and with this in mind my attention was drawn to a fully-rigged craft making, 'heavy weather' off Pill Creek. Looking through a pair of opera glasses, although the magnification was not high, I could see she was a ship's whaler, with fore, main, and mizzen set. These boats are strong, eighteen or twenty feet long, and were carried on board large naval vessels where they were used for crew training, and taking part in fleet regattas.

I gave Dad a running commentary of the whaler's progress, and remember saying "she will be in trouble when off the mouth, its gusting hard there".

The naval crew were probably on their way back to Falmouth after a 'run' ashore, and they had a dilemma, she was not fitted with an engine and the main sail had been reefed. Lowering all the sails and rowing was not wise, they would have quickly found themselves ashore at St Just in Roseland. There was no option but to head for shelter; Mylor Harbour would have been their best option.

Over the past four years we had sailed those waters, many times, we knew its power, moods, and tidal flows. We were at one with the boat, knew its, and our, limitations, when to turn for home, or shelter. And although local boatmen at that time, would not agree with me, we considered ourselves 'local Cornish,' and over the years since, I have often boasted, "I'm from the West Country, brought up in Cornwall"

We were, from the very beginning of the time we spent in that part of England, at one with the elements, and received, from the very best tutor, a grounding in seamanship that would never be forgotten. Bob in six years time would serve with distinction in the Royal Navy during the Korean conflict, and I, together with my family, have sailed long distances in all weather conditions, putting the skills gained as children to good use.

It was with this local knowledge that I viewed the progress of the whaler with apprehension. The wind had 'funnelled' into the mouth of Restronguet Creek, causing it to increase in velocity, and the whaler was fast approaching that area. She heeled well over, recovered momentarily, then over she went, throwing her crew into the water.

Although it was a Sunday I had already changed from my best 'new' long trousers into shorts, and had on a thick jumper. Dad had on a white shirt and tie. He rolled up his trousers, throwing on a jacket and we were off.

First the *Swordfish*, then into the *Steep Holmer*, in no time we cast off, engine running, throttle wide open, wind behind us, never had she moved at such a rate of knots.

We viewed the situation; there were about six men in the water swimming towards a large mooring buoy, where once ships had waited before sailing to Normandy.

Off Looe beach Mr Curnow, whom I knew, was making speed towards the men in the water. He had yellow-painted oyster boat, known at the time as a Quay Punt, fitted with a powerful Kelvin engine. He arrived at the area where the men were in the water, ahead of us.

We were about one hundred yards away, when we saw one of the sailors who had been separated from the others. He was face down in the water and splashing his arms. Under normal circumstances the correct way would have been to go down wind and turn, allowing the wind to slow the boat down, however every second counted, the sooner we had him aboard the better chance he had.

I stood up in the bow giving directions with the boat hook, left, right – as I have said before, the *Steep Holmer* had no gear box, just direct drive, so we had to judge the exact moment we would have to stop the engine and drift. We would have to have enough headway to reach him, too little or too much, would involve restarting the engine and making a second attempt.

Dad timed it exactly, shorting the spark plugs with a screwdriver at exactly the right moment; just enough headway to give us steerage. We were in luck, the chap was now almost completely submerged but he had on a pair of waterproof dungarees with braces which had enough air trapped inside to give him some buoyancy. I hooked the braces with the boat hook, and with one foot on the gunnels, in order to stop myself being dragged overboard, used him as a sea anchor slowing us down. Now the hard part, getting this dead weight on board.

We both stood on the gunnels and 'floated' him aboard, he was too far gone to help. However the seawater pouring aboard gave him a lift and we were like seamen up aloft in the old clipper sailing days. Clawing at his waterlogged clothing hand over hand, we tugged, floating, rolling, heaving until unceremoniously he fell face down over the centre seat. Blue in the face, he was violently sick in the bilges, which by that time contained a fair amount of the Fal estuary.

We then headed back towards home, Dad steering, me pumping out the bilges, while our water-logged friend coughed himself back to life. Mr Curnow drew alongside and two of the rescued sailors jumped aboard to take care of their colleague.

Because this was the last time we would use the *Steep Holmer*, my memory of the return trip is still clear. She punched her way into the wind, her little engine sounding like a sewing machine, there was no dodging the spray. Dad, dressed in a white shirt, tie and jacket, was wet through, and had it not been for the seriousness of our mission, I'm sure he would have been singing. 'Tom Bowling'.

We were not the only ones there that day, there were five others, if not in the flesh, then – to me – they were there in spirit, and our thoughts. Grandpop Harding would be reliving his uncanny dream of six years ago, now watching over his son and grandson. He would be a proud of us.

Mark, who had taught us the basics of seamanship and had set us on the right course which had seen us through many adventures, would be there, most certainly he was in the knowledge that he had passed on.

Three American sailors were also in our thoughts. We had realised how hard it was to pull a fully-clothed man into a boat at sea level, to do so from a landing craft would just have been just about impossible, and sadly, for them, it was.

Lots of hot drinks, and a couple of bottles of mead later, having dried out a little, transport arrived to take the Jolly Jack Tars back to Falmouth. Mr Curnow towed the whaler to Looe Beach, from where later, she was taken back to her ship. Pity, we would have loved to put her through her paces, weather permitting.

A restored engine of the type fitted in Steep Holmer.

A while later Dad was in the garden, he knew that one day the question would be asked and I know he had an answer ready.

"Why?" I asked, "was my name not in the papers, and mentioned in the letter you received about the rescue."

He stuck out his chest and said, "Well son it's like this, there's a seafaring tradition, the captain takes the rap if anything goes wrong, therefore it's only right that he takes the glory. And I was the skipper after all." So he was, he had seen to it that there was food on the table, given us freedom, and like so many others at that time, helped to keep the RAF equipped with aircraft. He died a relatively young man.

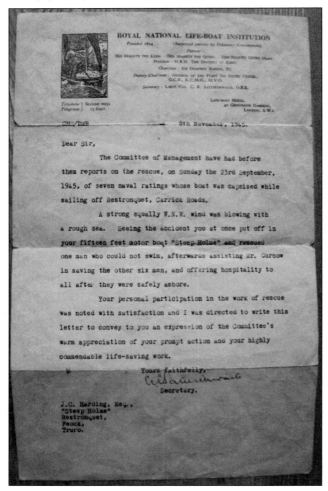

Letter of commendation addressed to the author's father from the RNLI for his part in rescuing seven naval ratings.

The *Steep Holmer* was sold. The end of the *Swordfish* was not only sad it was a mystery; we had intended to let Ted and Terry have her. She was found one morning, smashed to bits on the rocks.

On the previous night there had been a strong wind but nothing like the many storms she had ridden out before. I sat alone on the shore which was strewn with sections of her, and thought of her life, our boat, which like all others had a soul.

There's no doubt she started life as a ship's boat, lightly constructed from pine which had grown near the Arctic circle where for three months of the year it would be dark, and for three months of the year the sun never set. Branches would be covered in snow for much of the time, an environment which gave the timber its strength.

Her straight-grained pine planks were fastened with the finest copper nails, and as Cornwall at that time produced much of the world's copper, there is a strong possibility that the nails had now 'returned home'.

Her strong gunnels and large bronze rings – fore and aft – were designed to take her weight as she was lifted aboard her parent vessel, a schooner or brigantine perhaps. Together they would sail along John Masefield's, 'Gulls Way and Whale's Way.'

What a life she must have had, what stories she could have told, until, just when she thought that her life would slowly end on a mud bank near Truro City, she was resurrected.

Her new captain and crew would be pale-faced children with dark rings under their eyes, and a look in those eyes that could be construed as fear. That boat would take those children, and over the next five years turn them into young adults, providing them with an ample supply of fresh fish, fresh air and exercise. Their bodies and minds would develop, hair would become white through fresh air, sea water, and the sun. Blisters on their hands and backsides would be replaced by toughened skin.

Through blue sea and pitch darkness they would sail together, sometimes singing, often laughing, and once or twice quietly drifting, alone with just their thoughts, isolated from reality, which in my view is not a bad thing to do, for children of all ages.

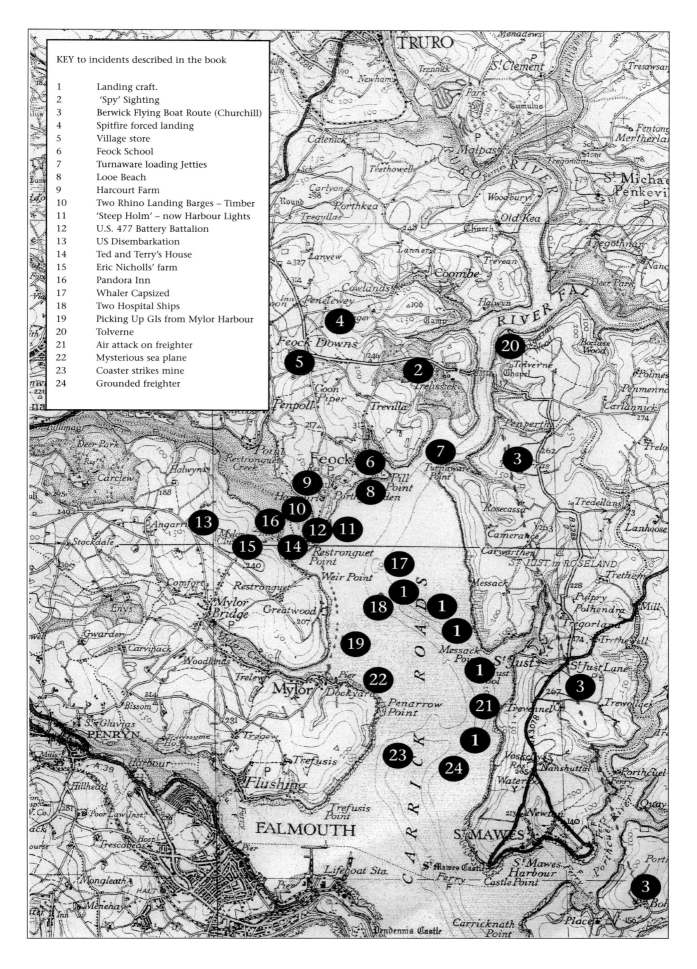

KEY to incidents described in the book

1	Landing craft.
2	'Spy' Sighting
3	Berwick Flying Boat Route (Churchill)
4	Spitfire forced landing
5	Village store
6	Feock School
7	Turnaware loading Jetties
8	Looe Beach
9	Harcourt Farm
10	Two Rhino Landing Barges – Timber
11	'Steep Holm' – now Harbour Lights
12	U.S. 477 Battery Battalion
13	US Disembarkation
14	Ted and Terry's House
15	Eric Nicholls' farm
16	Pandora Inn
17	Whaler Capsized
18	Two Hospital Ships
19	Picking Up GIs from Mylor Harbour
20	Tolverne
21	Air attack on freighter
22	Mysterious sea plane
23	Coaster strikes mine
24	Grounded freighter

Chapter 16

SIXTY-FIVE YEARS LATER

The fields, the orchard, and the woods at Restronguet point have today been replaced with fine looking houses, each with large, beautifully kept gardens, although I haven't seen any rabbits, other wildlife is there in abundance.

The ferry across to Pandora ceased operating many years ago. Yachts and other craft are moored and slipways have been built along that stretch of coast where in times now past a ship's boat with a silver sail, and a motor boat without a gearbox, reigned.

During the winter months, oyster fishermen still earn their living in the Carrick Roads. In the summertime, yachts with brightly-coloured sails are a sight to behold.

The stars are not as bright as they were, however, it is but a short car trip to the Lizard or the Land's End areas, and there on a clear night it is still possible to plant a memory.

The house we lived in is still there, just as it was all those years ago. Tall trees now stand where once oats grew and children played. There is nothing to show for the time we spent there. But wait! 'Our tree,' from where we had a grandstand view of things has gone, but just where Percy lived in his luxury sty, an oak tree grows, about sixty or so years old. Did his snout miss one of the acorns we gave him?

For readers who might one day visit the area covered by this book for the first time, I offer the following tour guide. By far the best way, in my opinion, would be to take a river boat trip from Falmouth.

After cruising through the open area of Carrick Roads, you will enter the deep green waters of the River Fal. To the right Turnaware disembarkation point will be pointed out to you by the knowledgeable crew. From here battalions of fighting men boarded landing craft before setting off for Normandy. Final remnants of jetties, and seaweed covered metal can still be seen there on the shore, to remind us of their presence and departure.

The quietness of the area is apparent to all who visit, disturbed only by the birds. The cuckoo can be heard in the springtime, and the grey heron stands motionless on the shore.

It is rare today that one can return to an area almost seventy years after leaving, and find it

Looking towards Turnaware.

A modern aerial photograph taken looking north over Carrick Roads with Restronguet Point in the left foreground. This was the superb background to the author's childhood

exactly the same as it was when a child. This is one such place, nothing has changed and happily is unlikely to do so, well, well, into the future. It is owned and managed by the National Trust. I pray that it will remain that way forever.

For me, this wooded area is not only one of the most beautiful and peaceful areas in the world, it is more than that, much more, it is a living memorial, a memorial to men who spent their last days camped there before D Day. They left with Cornish soil on their boots and washed it off wading ashore on the beaches of Normandy.

Many visitors today are convinced that distant voices can be heard here. It is a long-held dream of mine that one day a small church will be constructed here on the shore from Cornish granite, along with a seat made from a baulk of American oak. The site would be visible from the estuary and accessible from a small boat.

Engraved on a plaque inside, for those wishing to be alone with their thoughts, I envisage an engraved stone, bearing the following inscription.

In English, 'From here they left.'

And in French, '*D'ici ils sont venu.*' ("From here they came")

I was fortunate on one of my visits to have met Sheilagh Banner, who, as the daughter of the local Parish Council Chairman, unveiled just inland from the beach a commemoration stone that records the events of June 1944. Sheilagh has written a moving poem titled 'Turnaware'; she has kindly given permission to print it here.

TURNAWARE

Musty Damp crumble of autumn leaves,
Last wash of dimpsy light, as the day dies,
*   there is silence.*
But come again in spring,
When waves of bluebells, breakdown hill.
Come in the evening, and listen
Round the concrete remains of huts long
*   decayed.*
Faint shouts, a whistle of soldiers, soon to die.
Their tomorrow brings terror, crushing,
*   consuming,*
Acrid death, fear beyond imagining an end
*   of life.*
These woods held their last night,
Hidden and sweet under soft green beach leaves
*   and sentry moon, and holds it still.*

The memorial commemorating the D Day embarkation from Turnaware.

A sign on the road down to Tolverne, a reminder, to all who pass. Photo by kind permission of P. Newman

Further up the winding river at Tolverne is situated one of the best kept secrets of the preparations for the invasion of Normandy. Although at the time we as children prided ourselves that we 'knew it all,' and 'had seen it all', the planners were just that bit smarter. Hidden from view, unknown to us, a road was built through a wooded area where tanks and heavy equipment was hidden, impossible to see from low-flying aircraft, or from the river (and by children who had a sixth sense in such things!). So tight was security that my father who spent two nights a week at the River Patrol headquarters, which was situated at the end of the road, never once mentioned anything about it, of

Above and right: *The last remnants of the US army presence on the beach at Turnaware.*

Tanks disembarking from an LST on a Normandy beach.

the preparations taking place, or of tanks and equipment, hidden by day, travelling down to the slipways in the cover of total darkness where they would be loaded on to LSTs.

Landing here at the little thatched inn, tucked away in the trees, visitors can touch history. It's there that the River Patrol had their headquarters, and where over the years Peter Newman and his wife Elizabeth, have devoted so much effort maintaining a living memorial of historical importance. It's there on the slipway they have personally had a plaque placed, visible from the river, touchable to all who step ashore.

Many American ex-servicemen, now in their twilight years, still cross the Atlantic Ocean to pay homage to their 'Buddies' who only crossed once.

Peter Newman recalls an occasion when, an elderly American veteran returned to this area to pay homage; however on arrival at the scene that held so many memories, he became too emotional to go ashore.

The plaque erected by Paul and Elizabeth Newman.

For them, I include here the numbers of some of the LSTs who loaded tanks and equipment at Tolverne: US512; US56; US212; US7; US326; US197; US393; US5; US292; US497; US307; US61 and US54. There were many more.

More men men and equipment pour ashore from LSTs in the weeks following D Day.

Rhinos loaded with heavy equipment being towed ashore in Normandy.

Above: *A peaceful scene on the river as it meanders towards Truro.* Below: *The author's sketch of Truro City (so called in memory of his American 'Buddies) as it was during the war.*

In the sketch above a story is held. To the right, just out of sight, is where the prefabricated sections of Rhinos were landed having been brought across the Atlantic in liberty ships. Unloaded from the ships into barges moored near King Harry Ferry, the sections were then brought to Truro quay from where they were taken by six-wheel US lorries to a site near Malpas to be assembled. Towed to Normandy on D Day+1, tanks and heavy equipment was taken ashore on these flat-bottomed pontoons before the Mulberry harbours became operational. A vital part of the invasion strategy. The quay at Truro had never before, or since, played a major role, on such a scale.

In the sketch on the previous page I have placed, alongside the quay, a coastal smack. The crew have just finished unloading the cargo of road stone that was used to build the roads that carried the tanks and heavy equipment.

Sailing along the coast in waters frequented by enemy U-boats, and in constant danger of attack from the air, the experienced civilian crews of these coastal smacks, some as young as fifteen years of age, used the winds and tides to bring their cargoes to the heart of the areas where it would be urgently required. Stone and coal from South Wales, phosphates for the farming industry, and grain brought directly to the waterside mill, saving precious petrol and leaving the narrow roads clear for military use. These little ships, in the last years of their era, are fondly remembered by the privileged few.

The doubled-ended boat in the bottom left corner of the sketch is the *Swordfish*. She had been sold for ten pounds and on 24 May 1941 was taken down the River Fal to begin a new life.

The large 1930s white building seen in the sketch is HTP Motors, which also played an important role during the war years. It was in this factory, previously a garage and motor mechanics workshop, that Spitfire wings, flaps and tail sections were repaired. Local men and women, some with little or no prior engineering experience, were recruited and trained in this vital war work.

The following sequence of photographs, kindly provided by the Royal Cornwall Museum in Truro show in remarkable clarity some of the work undertaken. The author's captions provide interesting stories and information, including details of a remarkable personal link, relating to these fascinating pictures.

If ever there was a picture that told a story then this must be it. A teenager at the HTP factory repairs a section of a Spitfire that had crash landed during the Battle of Britain. Here she is proudly applying her stamp – her 'signature' – that identifies the repair as being hers. In less than a week the aircraft will be back in the skies.

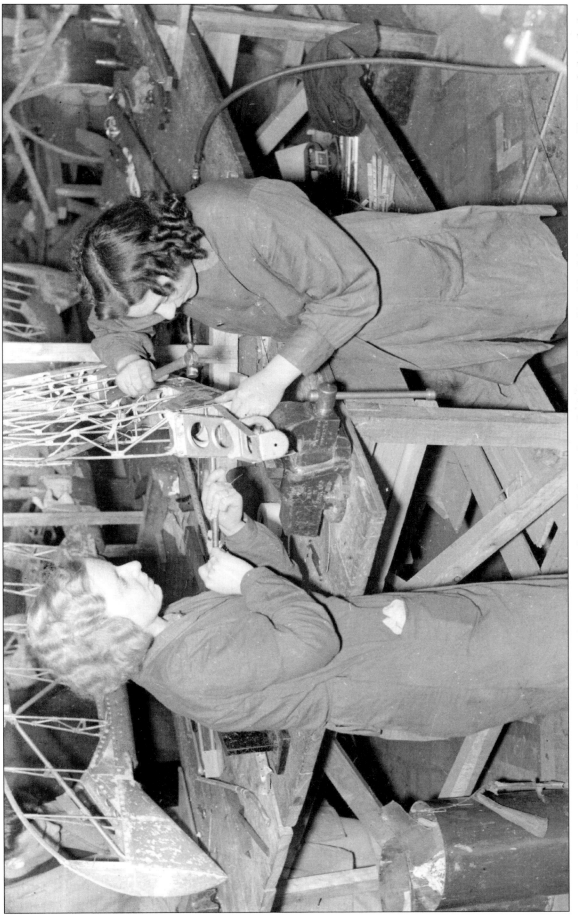

The innocence of youth? We know better, you and I, Mercia Marchant. We know that when you and your friend in this photograph were on Fire Watch duty during the war you both went home to bed in the early hours, taking the keys of the factory with you. Oversleeping you both ran through the streets of Truro in your pyjamas to let the queue of waiting workmen into work. Your secret is safe with me Mercia however; passing your motor cycle test at 75 years of age will not clean the slate. Seriously, you and your friend Marjory Hoskins boosted moral at HTP Motors.

Inside the HTP motors factory in Truro showing the large numbers of people employed in the repair of aircraft.

Where motor mechanics once serviced British marques such as Austin, MG and Wolesley, men and women now worked at massive jigs such as that seen centre left where wing sections and tailplanes of Spitfires were repaired.

The woman on the left strips down an aerilon from a damaged aircraft while her colleagues carry out repairs.

And as the author's story comes to a close this photograph provided the final coincidence. In researching photographs at the Royal Cornwall Museum in Truro he came across this sequence of photographs of HTP Motors. This was where his father worked during the war, overseeing the vital war work in the repair of damaged aircraft, and to his delight the author was able to identify the man standing on the far right in this photograph as his father.

Chapter 17

LOOSE ENDS

The house where we lived at Elburton, Plymouth has been extensively rebuilt, the cellar where we sheltered from the bombing is now a modern kitchen. The large steps at the rear that saved us from much of the bomb blast have been demolished, and used to raise the level of the rear garden. However, a suggestion was made to my sister Anne and myself that we should call on the adjoining property.

The couple who now live there were very helpful, and gave us permission to have a look in the cellar. We could never have imagined the sight before our eyes. Many years ago the rear section of the cellar was boarded off and had not been entered since.

A small removable hatch had been built to allow access for emergency entry, but never used. We were given permission, and help, to remove the hatch. A torch revealed a time warp of emotional memories. The rear of this adjoining house, received similar blast damage. Large stones had been blown against the adjoining wall, and they were still there. With the aid of a torch we were taken back through time. The photograph which I took records the atmosphere. It was obtained through luck more than photographic skill.

No, I didn't get the silver cigarette lighter back. Jo and Hank wrote to us until the end of the war, and their last letters were received as they were about to leave France, bound for the United States. I would, have liked to know where it ended its journeys. Of course, I pray that it doesn't lie somewhere in foreign soil. No, I prefer to think of one or the other of the following final resting places for it.

Somewhere in America perhaps there is a playground where a boy, or a girl for that matter, proudly shows it to their friends, "My granddad was given this by some English kid as he was leaving to fight in France."

I have news for them, "I was that English Kid, and will willingly give a model of RMS *Queen Elizabeth* for that lighter now. Or. Does a French lady, now like me in her twilight years, still have the wonderful gift of memory, and like to reminisce about the days of youthful joy, combined with the sadness of war. Does she open the top drawer of her dressing table, take out a silver cigarette lighter from its silk handkerchief wrapping, hold it for the thousandth time, and with a gentle smile whisper, *"J'étais si jeune et innocent jadis et était Seulment un garçon"* – "I was so young and innocent then, and he was but a boy".

Bomb damaged revealed in the cellar in Elburton, Plymouth almost 70 years later.

The view today from 'Harbour Lights', peace and tranquility. A painting by David Parry. Author's Collection

Morning at King Harry Ferry.

Devoran Creek, taken on 19 March 2010 just yards from where GI personnel were camped at Restronguet Point in the spring of 1944. It is this view, unchanged over 65 years, that many would remember; the morning mists, and the sunsets.

The author's childhood friend, Ted, was given this flag by the Americans who were camped at Restronguet point. One of them stuck it to the mudguard of Ted's bicycle. Ted had the foresight to keep it safe in his Sunday School Bible where it has survived all these years.